How We Cope with Digital Technology

Synthesis Lectures on Human-Centered Informatics

Editor
John M. Carroll, *Penn State University*

Human-Centered Informatics (HCI) is the intersection of the cultural, the social, the cognitive, and the aesthetic with computing and information technology. It encompasses a huge range of issues, theories, technologies, designs, tools, environments and human experiences in knowledge work, recreation and leisure activity, teaching and learning, and the potpourri of everyday life. The series publishes state-of-the-art syntheses, case studies, and tutorials in key areas.

Conceptual Models: Core to Good Design
Jeff Johnson and Austin Henderson
2011

Geographical Design: Spatial Cognition and Geographical Information Science
Stephen C. Hirtle
2011

User-Centered Agile Methods
Hugh Beyer
2010

Experience-Centered Design: Designers, Users, and Communities in Dialogue
PeterWright and John McCarthy
2010

Experience Design: Technology for All the Right Reasons
Marc Hassenzahl
2010

Designing and Evaluating Usable Technology in Industrial Research: Three Case Studies
Clare-Marie Karat and John Karat
2010

Interacting with Information
Ann Blandford and Simon Attfield
2010

Designing for User Engagement: Aesthetic and Attractive User Interfaces
Alistair Sutcliffe
2009

Context-Aware Mobile Computing: Affordances of Space, Social Awareness, and Social Influence
Geri Gay
2009

Studies ofWork and theWorkplace in HCI: Concepts and Techniques
Graham Button andWes Sharrock
2009

Semiotic Engineering Methods for Scientific Research in HCI
Clarisse Sieckenius de Souza and Carla Faria Leitão
2009

Common Ground in Electronically Mediated Conversation
Andrew Monk
2008

How We Cope with Digital Technology
Phil Turner

ISBN: 978-3-031-01073-6   print
ISBN: 978-3-031-02201-2   ebook

DOI 10.1007/978-3-031-02201-2

A Publication in the Morgan & Claypool Publishers series
SYNTHESIS LECTURES ON HUMAN-CENTERED INFORMATICS
Lecture #18
Series Editor: John M. Carroll, Penn State University

Series ISSN   1946-7680 Print   1946-7699 Electronic

How We Cope with
Digital Technology

Phil Turner
Edinburgh Napier University

SYNTHESIS LECTURES ON HUMAN-CENTERED INFORMATICS #18

ABSTRACT

Digital technology has become a defining characteristic of modern life. Almost everyone uses it, we all rely on it, and many of us own a multitude of devices. What is more, we all expect to be able to use these technologies "straight out the box." This lecture discusses how we are able to do this without apparent problems.

We are able to use digital technology because we have learned to cope with it. "To cope" is used in philosophy to mean "absorbed engagement," that is, we use our smart phones and tablet computers with little or no conscious effort. In human-computer interaction this kind of use is more often described as intuitive. While this, of course, is testament to improved design, our interest in this lecture is in the human side of these interactions. We cope with technology because we are familiar with it.

We define familiarity as the readiness to engage with technology which arises from being repeatedly exposed to it—often from birth. This exposure involves the frequent use of it and seeing people all around us using it every day. Digital technology has become as common a feature of our everyday lives as the motor car, TV, credit card, cutlery, or a dozen other things which we also use without conscious deliberation. We will argue that we cope with digital technology in the same way as we do these other technologies by means of this everyday familiarity.

But this is only half of the story. We also regularly support or scaffold our use of technology. These scaffolding activities are described as "epistemic actions" which we adopt to make it easier for us to accomplish our goals. With digital technology these epistemic actions include appropriating it to more closer meet our needs.

In summary, coping is a situated, embodied, and distributed description of how we use digital technology.

KEYWORDS

coping, familiarity, prior knowledge, epistemic actions, scaffolding

Contents

Callouts

Figures and Tables

Acknowledgments

Sincere thanks go to my reviewers, Professor Giuseppe Riva and Professor Erik Stolterman, for their constructive and perceptive comments on the content of this book; to my editor, Diane Cerra, for her cheerful management of the process, and to my wife Susan, who has listened (relatively) patiently to many rehearsals of the argument presented here.

CHAPTER 1

Introduction

The use of digital technology is now a major part of our lives, and Human-Computer Interaction (HCI) has created a whole raft of models and descriptions that tell us what we use it for. We also know why we use this technology rather than that technology; where and when we use it (at home, on the move, at work) and how frequently we use it. In short, we have a fairly comprehensive picture of its role in modern life, except to say, that there is no account of *how* we use it.

The aim of this lecture is do just that, to offer an account of *how* we use digital technology by drawing upon psychological, philosophical, cognitive science, and human-computer interaction research.

We start from where we find ourselves, surrounded by a heterogeneous mix of technologies being used by a very diverse population typically without much difficulty. This is all the more remarkable as only some thirty years ago researchers struggled to find a way to present what were then unfamiliar technologies to people. The desktop metaphor was invented as were a host of input and output devices. We created psychological models of how people thought about it. We worried about training, the writing of manuals, and of user acceptance. Now, of course, we worry about the effects of overusing technology and even "addiction." Surveys reported in the popular press tell us that people "can't live without their phones," prefer their phones to their children, and that the number of mobile computing devices is about to exceed the number of people on the planet. We also learn that these technologies are making us stupid, violent, or obese (or all three). Whether or not this is mere hyperbole, the simple truth is that for many of us the routine use of digital technology is an everyday fact of life.

So, *how* do we use digital technology? It will be argued that we *cope* with it. This is not the coping of solicitude. Instead, borrowing the term from philosophy, it is taken to mean "absorbed engagement." Used in this way, coping is a description of how we broadly deal with the world and everything it comprises.

We have learned to cope with digital technology in the same ways that we have learned to cope with cutlery, washing machines, automatic bank tellers, TVs, motorcars, and so forth (but we exclude operating a nuclear power station, flying commercial airliners, and other such complex, safety critical activities from this list). We have learned to cope with these technologies because they surround us, because we may have been instructed in their use, because we have watched others use them, because we have to, and because we want to. We cope with digital technology without conscious deliberation or reflection, indeed, we might say *intuitively*. While coping does not rely on conscious deliberation, it is nonetheless adaptive, that is, we respond flexibly to the demands of the situation.

Further we also *scaffold* our coping with heuristics, short-cuts, and a whole host of "work-arounds" and supporting behaviours. These we collectively describe as *epistemic actions* (Kirsh and Maglio, 1994). These actions help us achieve our goals by making them less demanding. While examples of epistemic actions are readily identified, as we discuss in Chapter 4, coping with digital technology does, however, differ from the use of other technologies in one important respect. We frequently personalise it, configure it, and in doing so we make it better suited to the ways in which we want to use it. In short, we appropriate it. This is not to suggest that appropriation is confined to digital technology but it does seem to be one of its defining characteristics. In recent years research into how we appropriate technology has grown dramatically. Appropriation is now recognised to encompass not only personalisation and configuration, but includes re-use, sustainability, and what has been described as "ensoulment." There is even growing interest in designing for appropriation (though this is deemed by some as oxymoronic; Dix, 2007). However, for the purposes of this lecture, we will treat appropriation in a very specific way, namely, as a form of epistemic action involved with making digital technology easier to use and more appropriate to how we want to use it.

1.1   DIGITAL NATIVES

Accepting that digital technology is one of the defining features of our everyday lives has prompted some to consider what effect this has had on us. This kind of discussion varies widely between the utopian and dystopian, the enthusiastic and the horrified, the popular and the academic. Nicholas Carr, for example, has famously asked, "Is Google making us stupid" (Carr, 2008). By "Google," of course, he intends the Web as a whole and goes on to wonder about the effect digital technology has on our ability to think, read, and remember (Carr, 2010). Similarly McGonagall (2011) has published astonishing statistics about how much time people spend playing video games while proposing that such games provide a panacea for the ills of everyday life as they are a source of "positive experiences."

One area of real concern is the effect of interactive technology on the cognitive and emotional development of children and young people. While this is undoubtedly important, it is not the focus here. Instead we note that early, repeated, everyday exposure of children to digital technology results in their familiarity with it. Figure 1.1 is an image of two-year-old Ella. Ella loves pretending to be a dinosaur, loves being read stories, and using her parents' iPad. The picture of Ella is not intended to convey something about the hours she might spend in front of a screen (to the exclusion of other activities) but that technologies like the iPad are simply a part of her everyday life along with her toy sheep. She is becoming familiar with technology and learning to cope with it as a matter of course. This is unremarkable and no different in kind to learning to read, getting dressed, completing a jigsaw, and so forth.

Figure 1.1: Two-year-old Ella using an Apple iPad.

Toy manufacturers (e.g., BRIO) also ensure that children's familiarity with this kind of technology begins early. They offer "my first mobile phone" (a toy) which is said to be suitable for children aged 10 months and over which is more or less at the threshold of the child's first spoken word.

In practice, of course, children really do not have much of a choice about this as they find themselves being "thrown", to use Heidegger's term, into a world filled with this technology (Heidegger's Obscure Terminology).

One popular characterisation of the consequences of this early and repeated exposure to technology is Prensky's (2001) "digital native", and although he is specifically describing students, many of his remarks may generalise to the wider population. He writes, "Today's students represent the first generations (sic) to grow up with this new technology. They have spent their entire lives surrounded by and using computers, videogames, digital music players, video cams, cell phones, and all the other toys and tools of the digital age. Today's average college grads have spent less than 5,000 hours of their lives reading, but over 10,000 hours playing video games […] Computer games, email, the Internet, cell phones and instant messaging are integral parts of their lives." Prensky goes on to argue that these "digital natives" may be so expert with digital technology that they may prove to be impossible to teach by "non-natives." While finding students difficult to teach is a complaint rediscovered by every generation of lecturers, more interestingly he observes that differences in the use of language between generations may be the real issue. We discuss the importance of language in Sections 2.5 and 4.6.

Heidegger's Obscure Terminology

Ready-to-Hand

Ready-to-hand-ness is probably Heidegger's most familiar expression to HCI specialists. The current treatment of the term is to regard it as simply meaning handy or handiness (**Verbeek, 2005**, p. 79) . However we will begin be treating it as meaning "available."

Dreyfus and Wrathall (**2005**, p. 4) in their introduction to a collection of essays on Heidegger write, "we first encounter worldly things as available. Something is encountered as available when: it is defined in terms of its place in a context of equipment, typical activities in which it is used, and typical purposes and goals for which it is used, and it lends itself to such use readily and easily without need for reflection. *The core case of availability is an item of equipment that we know how to use and that transparently lends itself to use."* The italicised sentence gets to the nub of readiness-to-hand for the current discussion. When we see an item of technology (a) we know how to use it and (b) we become absorbed in that use. If the technologies meet these criteria then it is being experienced as being ready-to-hand (RTH).

Availability (another near synonym for RTH) also means proximal. Availability refers to the experience of using the technology and not to the technology per se, it is not a design feature. Readiness-to-hand is also a recognition that we do not encounter technology as discrete objects but as part of a meaningful network of things we can use, exploit, or engage with. This means that the expression "item of technology" as used above, is not quite right.

Present-at-Hand

Experiencing technology as being present-at-hand stands in contrast with readiness-to-hand. Rather than encountering the world directly and immediately this is rather like a scientist standing back and looking at the world objectively—perhaps through a microscope. This is the world *objectively present* (**Verbeek, 2005**). When we encounter something as present-at-hand it is in terms of the bare facts; we are not involved. Being present-at-hand is not the way in which we usually encounter the world, so is seen as somewhat secondary.

Dasein

The word Dasein is derived from *da-sein*, which literally means being-there or there-being, though this is not a translation with which Heidegger was happy. It has also been taken to mean "existence" and "human being." In his *Being and Time* (**1927/1962**, p. 27) Heidegger writes, "This entity which each of us is himself … we shall denote by the term Dasein." The argument is that the identity of each of us is essentially indeterminate and necessarily contingent. Our identities, for Heidegger, are a consequence of our "*know-how*." We are surgeons because we can conduct surgery, actors because we can act, celebrities because we are celebrated.

Throwness (Geworfenheit)

The concept of throwness, along with ready-to-hand and present-at-hand, are the three Heideggerian terms which Winograd and Flores introduced to the HCI community in the 1980s. While throwness has a particularly opaque formal definition, they offer a much more useful illustration of the term. They invite us to imagine that we are chairing a meeting. We must allow people to speak, take a vote, cut off speakers as required, keep the meeting on topic, and so forth. Winograd and Flores (**1986**) observe from this example of being thrown in this situation that: (i) we cannot avoid acting—as chairs we are thrown into action; (ii) we cannot step back and reflect—we are thrown back on our instincts and must deal with issues as they arise.

In short we cannot act like dispassionate scientists weighing the evidence but as people thrown into real-world, evolving situations (**ibid**, pp. 33-36).

1.2   UNRULY, COMPLEX TECHNOLOGY

Digital technology has indeed become ubiquitous but in a manner which does not quite match the original conception as articulated by Weiser. He described it as the seamless embedding of information processing into everyday objects and activities, writing that "the most profound technologies are those that disappear. They weave themselves into the fabric of everyday life until they are indistinguishable from it" (Weiser, 1991). While this fabric has indeed been populated by all manner of digital technology, to suggest that it is seamless would be optimistic. Since Weiser's insight, a number of attempts have been made to realise this. Weiser and Brown (1996) have proposed designing what they describe as "Calm Technology" which, "informs but doesn't demand our focus or attention" while Wisneski and his colleagues (1998) have proposed "ambient displays" which make use of existing spaces to afford interaction, and Tolmie et al. (2002) have proposed "Unremarkable Computing" which aims at encouraging designers to support the mundane, everyday routines of life with digital technology.

In reality, rather than these proposed seamless, embedded technologies, we have the problem of interaction complexity (Janlert and Stolterman, 2010) arising from artefact ecologies (Jung et al., 2008; Ryan et al., 2009). Bødker and Klokmose (2012a, p. 448) tell us that the last decade has seen our ecologies transformed from the simple, perhaps comprising a single personal computer (PC), to the complex made up from "music players, gaming consoles, smartphones, PCs, entertainment systems, interactive walls etc." Their interest, however, is in the seams between technologies and not in seamlessness per se. These discussions serve to highlight the everyday nature of technological ubiquity as unruliness rather than smooth embeddedness.

1.3   MONDAY, MONDAY

A typical Monday morning at work for me begins with switching on my computer. After it has booted, I enter my user name and password. The next task of the day is to have a quick look at my email. A single click on the email icon and the application loads. New messages appear in bold, some may be flagged as urgent, and a number will have been routed to the trash in response to the rules I have created. While I am getting my papers together and making a cup of tea, the reminder system pops up and flags an event at 10.00 am. This also prompts me to check my calendar … and so on … This unremarkable description includes examples of automatic, habitual, and routine behaviour. Many of the tasks involve digital technology but others do not. We enter our network credentials, we use a computer mouse, we start applications, we make a cup of tea, we scan for un-read email, we gather papers together, and so forth automatically and with scarce a thought. This kind of description, which is boringly familiar to me, plays out in a multitude of variants. Perhaps, for others, the morning is centred around checking one's social media account or grabbing a quick video game before going to school. Irrespective of these differences, these routines and habits are the fabric of everyday life. This perspective is echoed by Agre who tells us that "everyday life is almost wholly routine …" which he defines as, "a frequently repeated pattern of interaction between an agent and its familiar environment" (1997, p. 107). We will discuss the nature of this familiarity in some detail in the next chapter.

1.4   THE HABITUAL NATURE OF EVERYDAY LIFE

William James (1890, p. 122) recognised the importance of habits, writing, "We must make automatic and habitual, as early as possible, as many useful actions as we can." He even suggested, perhaps a little unkindly, that "the young" will become mere walking bundles of habits and, of course, we were all young once. Dewey (1922, p. 178) adds that habits do not require conscious thought, writing, "we walk and read aloud, we get off and on street cars, we dress and undress, and do a thousand useful acts without thinking of them." These sentiments have been echoed by Pollard (2006) who writes that we often use "habit" as an explanation of everyday life, concluding his discussion by observing, "When we consider just how much of our lives we spend exercising habits, rather than subjecting our actions to deliberation [...] thought is very helpful when we are in novel or important circumstances, the rest of the time it rather gets in the way ... we only think when our habits give out" (p. 18). Pollard also asks us to consider how we acquire a habit. He invites us to imagine someone acquiring the habit φ. Initially, she is able to φ but not automatically; instead φ-ing requires thought and concentration. After repetition, φ-ing has become automatic, φ-ing has become part of what she does. Eventually φ-ing is not just second nature: it has become part of the bundle of habits which define her. So, for Pollard, habits begin as deliberate actions and through repetition they become automatic.

Stephen Turner (1994, p. 16) expands on this telling us that "Habit is a hybrid term, at once mentalistic and observational. The difference between habits and repetitive behaviours, or the distinction between habit and innate inclination or impulsive act is an aetiological one. To have a habit is to have a particular kind of mental cause operating." He goes on, "Habits are acquired, and there is something which persists between manifestations, a mental trace. The same kind of reasoning that we grant in the case of habits with directly visible manifestations, that there is an invisible "mental" element by virtue of which the visible pattern of behaviour persists, may be extended to those "habits of mind", that we can identify and speak of only indirectly, through complex inferences." Norros (2005) offers an alternate description of habits from a semiotic perspective. She regards habits as having three interlinked characteristics. The first of these is the repetitious regularity of behaviour. It is this aspect that we emphasise in our everyday use of the term. The second characteristic of habits is that they "offer[s] the possibility to express meaning in action" (p. 388). She continues, habits are the way of being for most of us and can be understood in terms of *personal habit*. We have individual, habitual ways of thinking, speaking, behaving, and so forth. What is being repeated is our way of *coping* with the world. This repetition of the message is the third and final defining characteristic of a habit in that it has a reflexive component.

In summary, habits are useful; most of our everyday behaviours comprise habits; habits have to be learned, and habits are regularities of behaviour. But simply to describe our use of digital technology as habitual is not enough. Coping, as will be argued, offers a much richer account of use and as such the opportunity of greater insight into our everyday use of technology.

1.5   COPING, COMPORTMENT, AND COGNITION

As we have already said, coping as a description of our dealings with the world is drawn from the philosophical literature (e.g., Heidegger, 1927/1962; Dreyfus, 1991; Valera, 1992; Wheeler, 2005).

Although differing in detail, these accounts emphasise our smooth, unreflective, non-representational dealings with the world. Examples of coping include being able to eat a meal, make a cup of tea, type at a keyboard, swipe the surface of a mobile phone with a finger, drive a car and, of course, the philosophers' favourite example, being skilled with a hammer. It is also emphasised that coping does not rely on explicit knowledge or an underlying cognitive representation but is better thought of as comportment which is "an according with" the task or technology in hand. Coping may be thought of as "cognition in action" and as such is a little at odds with the traditional or classical accounts of our use of digital technology.

These accounts were largely predicated on some form of information processing paradigm. In general, it is supposed that we have a cognitive representation of the operation of the digital technology which we manipulate in order to formulate plans which in turn we execute (e.g., Card et al., 1983; Norman, 1983; 1988; John and Kieras, 1996). While these "mental model" approaches were once popular, they have less currency today. Classical cognition has, of course, been eclipsed by the appearance of various forms of extended, external, shared, embodied, distributed, and situated cognition hypotheses. These different accounts vary considerably but all would agree that cognition is neither confined to an individual brain nor limited to abstract deliberation.

Instead, cognition will be treated in this lecture primarily as the ability to function effectively in the world while recognising that it is embodied, situated and so forth. In many respects coping and cognition are one and the same but it must be emphasised that our primary focus is confined to how we successfully use digital technology.

Put another way, in only a generation we have gone from wondering how to get people to use this new and unfamiliar digital technology (focussing on technology acceptance and ease of use) to wondering how almost everyone seems to be able to use complex technology with such apparent ease.

1.6   ACTIONS TO SUPPORT COPING

From the description of coping we have considered so far, it might appear that we have reduced the typical person to little more than an automaton responding unthinkingly to the stimuli (and affordances) offered by digital technology. But this is not so. While coping describes most of our everyday use of digital technology it is not a complete account.

To coping we add a supporting role for the epistemic. For a definition of this we follow Goldman (1986, p. 13) who describes it as dealing with "affairs of the intellect", which include "[…] the entire canvas of topics the mind can address: the nature of man-made symbols and culture, and even the simple layout of objects in the immediate environment. The ways that minds do or should deal with these topics, individually or in concert, comprise the province of epistemology."

So, by the epistemic or the epistemological we do not just mean knowledge, as we also include those acts which are intended to make the technology easier to use, better suited to us, and as such accord with Kirsh and Maglio's (1994) definition of epistemic actions. Epistemic actions involve people changing their environment, their ways of working and making the technology itself more appropriate. Thus, just as we neatly stack dishes before we wash them, we store our files in folders (both electronic and paper) for ease of retrieval, we use timetables to maximise the chance of catching a train to work, and we operate multiple email accounts to manage work and home correspondence. Many of these actions are purely contingent, short-lived, and dynamic while others are well established. As we shall see in Chapter 4 examples of epistemic actions are myriad.

While it is recognised that coping and epistemic actions do not necessarily fit together philosophically (as will be also discussed in detail in Chapter 4) their successful union relies on their mutual availability. In short, coping must be able to access and exploit what the epistemic actions provide without "missing a beat", that is, there should be no need for conscious deliberation to make use of them. The parallel with the operation of affordances is both clear and intended.

Consider the following simple illustration of coping supported by epistemic actions: imagine one has a morning meeting in London for which we must catch the early morning flight. Not being at our best at 0500, we leave our keys and notes, mobile phone, wallet, and so forth in strategic locations to serve both as reminders to take them and as things we must take with us. We plan this in advance. Leaving keys and travel documents along the route we will take ensures that we will encounter them and take them with us. We scaffold "our going to the airport" coping with artefacts made deliberately proximal and available. Picking up these artefacts does not require deliberation but is intuitive: recognising our car keys does not require conscious thought, unlike remembering to pick them up from the drawer in the kitchen where they are usually kept. While these "breadcrumbs" are planned and deliberate, their use is intuitive, direct and immediate. So, having proposed that we cope with digital technology, a more complete description is to recognise that this coping is supported or "scaffolded" by a host of epistemic actions.

1.7   THIS LECTURE

The aim of this lecture is to describe the constituent and dynamic aspects of this formulation of coping and as such provide an account of how we use digital technology.

The ensuing chapters expand on the aspects of coping just introduced. We begin by arguing that we cope because we are familiar with digital technology and this familiarity is born of our habitual use of it and our early, frequent, and vicarious exposure to it. From there we move to a consideration of what is meant by coping from a number of complementary philosophical and psychological perspectives. Moving from coping, epistemic actions are described together how they serve to scaffold our coping. This lecture concludes with a discussion of how this account of coping fits with the main body of HCI.

CHAPTER 2

Familiarity

2.1 KEY POINTS

- Familiarity with digital technology comprises "know-how" (practical understanding) and involvement (that is, our use of technology is concernful in that it is neither detached nor disinterested).

- Familiarity with digital technology is acquired from multiple sources, including our everyday use of it, reading about it, and being instructed in its use. It is also acquired vicariously (e.g., from watching other people use it and from advertisements). This heterogeneity results in, for most people, a "collage" or patchwork of fragments of this or that rather than a neat, formal (mental) model.

- Most importantly, to be familiar with digital technology is to be ready to cope with it. When a new, must-have gadget appears, we expect to be able to use it without having to undertake a training course or having to read the manual. Instead we expect to unbox it and use it immediately relying on our "know-how."

- "Know-how" is tacit knowledge and as such does not lend itself to articulation. For example, I know how to type but I would struggle to tell someone how I do it.

- We are involved with technology because we want to own it, or we aspire to owning it, and increasingly, we have to use it as a requirement of our jobs or to access any number of services. Technology is also a statement of who we are, or would like to be seen as.

- To be unfamiliar with digital technology is to lack the practical skills to use it and to have no place for it in our everyday lives.

- Familiarity has an important, though under-researched, role in HCI. It is often associated with making sense of tasks or providing the basis of shared meaning.

2.2 DEFINING FAMILIARITY

Familiarity is a thorough knowledge of, or an intimacy with, something or someone. The etymology of the word indicates that it is from the same root as *family*, while for Heidegger, familiarity encompasses the ideas of involvement and understanding. So, to be familiar with something one must both be involved with it and understand it, and this indeed is consonant with the relationship one has with our families.

Applying this to digital technology is not quite as simple. While it is quite easy to equate *understanding* with our ability to use it effectively (Knowing-How and Knowing-That), it is more difficult to account for our involvement with it. For Heidegger involvement is an expression of care, not in the sense of solicitude, but one of being directed towards something and being responsive to it. We are concerned about, or make, technology an issue for ourselves.

Knowing-How and Knowing-That

Most people would agree that it was Gilbert Ryle, in his presidential address to the Aristotelian Society in November 1945, who first distinguished (in a philosophical sense) between *knowing-how* and *knowing-that*. After a wordy preamble he asks what does the expert chess player know that the novice does not. He suggests that the expert might be able to impart tricks, wrinkles, and tactical maxims (examples of knowing-that) but the novice is likely to continue to play stupidly as he is unable to apply these tricks because he lacks the *know-how* to do so. Most importantly Ryle argued that these two forms of knowledge are independent of each other but that we learn *how-to* before we learn *that*.

This distinction can be found across the HCI and cognitive science literature. Knowing-that is often called propositional knowledge, an example of which is that London is the capital of England. Knowing-how, in contrast, includes knowing how to type or ride a cycle, often referred to as tacit knowledge (**Polyani, 1983**).

While Ryle usually receives the credit for this distinction, the ancient Greeks actually made a three-way distinction. They identified *episteme*, usually translated as *knowledge*, while *techne* means *craft* or *art* (the root of our word technology), and the third, least known form, is *phronesis* or *practical wisdom* or *prudence*.

The episteme/techne distinction is roughly equivalent to the difference between knowing-that and knowing-how (respectively) but their relationship is not quite that simple (if it were, there would be little call for philosophy). As for phronesis, this has largely remained in obscurity until Flyvbjerg (**2001**) made a very strong case for its role in the social sciences.

This understanding-involvement structure allows us to equate familiarity with a readiness to cope (based on *know-how* and prior knowledge) and our involvement prompting us to engage with the technology itself.

Taking firstly, familiarity as the readiness to cope with digital technology, this is our "know-how." This aspect of familiarity also depends upon prior knowledge. Familiarity is the product of repeated exposure to technology and this prior knowledge is central to the successful use of both familiar and unfamiliar technology.

Familiarity is also an expression of our involvement with technology. Our involvement is the basis of our active exploration of and subsequent use of technology; our interest in it; and our engagement with it. Involvement is the ontological core of these behaviours and is ultimately why we aspire to own those expensive, little black boxes.

In order to underline the nature and importance of familiarity we then consider what it might be like to be unfamiliar with digital technology. For this we draw upon the findings of an extended study of a group of seniors learning to use computers.

Finally we consider familiarity's place within HCI proper. Familiarity has not received a great deal of sustained interest, however, it has been found to be an important factor in making sense of a task on both an individual and shared basis and the means by which our use of technology becomes automatic, in the sense of not requiring conscious thought.

2.3   READINESS TO COPE

Dreyfus (1991, p. 9) tells us that "Familiarity consists of dispositions to respond to situations in appropriate ways", this is to recognise that familiarity is the *readiness to cope* with technology. Familiarity may also be thought of as *comportment*. Comportment is a rather dated term outside of philosophical discourse but can still be found in expressions such as, "she comported herself with dignity" which might be read as "carried herself" or "held herself." Comportment might be understood as, "according with" and examples of this include "knowing" just how high to raise our feet when we climb a flight of stairs (e.g., Warren, 1984), and the way to shape our hands when picking up a cup of coffee, a cat, a small child, or a pay cheque. As comportment is a little unfamiliar it is worth pausing for a moment to consider the differences between it and the kind of knowledge structures that have been proposed to hold this kind of everyday knowledge.

Familiarity, as readiness to cope, sounds like an orienting schema or perhaps more like a script that might guide our actions. Schank and Abelson's (1977) proposed scripts, which like a schema or frame, are structures that describe a sequence of events in a given context and as such provide a readiness to respond to situations appropriately. A script comprises a set of "slots" with rules as to what can occupy those slots. This can be most easily seen in Schank and Abelson's most famous example, the restaurant script. This script describes how to behave in a variety of different restaurants by simply changing the contents of the "slots" from, say, Chinese to Indian and "order at the table" to "order at the counter" depending on the venue. They very neatly describe a script as, "a very boring little story." Scripts were one of a number of different attempts by Artificial Intelligence (AI) researchers to tackle the problem of representing real world knowledge and the comments we make here are broadly applicable to the other related proposals such as schemata and frames.

So how are these classically cognitive accounts different from comportment? They differ in at least three ways: firstly, scripts are described by their creators as stereotyped, simplified, and abstracted from the complexities of the real world. They offer little treatment of the situated (Suchman, 1987) and the embodied (e.g., Clark, 2008). They only appear to represent the world in miniature ("*microworlds*") for example, ordering dinner in a restaurant but without any suggestion of how your fellow dinners got there, or your partner's food allergy, or the dispute over the bill at the end of the evening. Secondly, and perhaps more importantly for the current discussion, while the scripts may describe where to order to dinner, they do not offer guidance on how to sit at a chair, how to make small talk, how eat soup, how to pour wine into a glass and then take a knowing sip. Scripts and other forms of representation can only represent knowledge that can be articulated, and familiarity cannot be captured in this way.

Finally, scripts, schemata, and frames[1] are static, though configurable, cognitive structures whereas familiarity is intrinsically dynamic. In all, familiarity is an example of *tacit* knowledge (Polyani, 1983).

In his *The Tacit Dimension*, Polyani tells us that "we can know more than we can tell" and it is this kind of knowing he calls, "tacit knowledge." For example, I am (personally) able to ride a bicycle, use chopsticks, touch type, find my way to the local railway station, and take a train to work because I am familiar with bicycles, chopsticks, keyboards, and the vagaries and everyday operation of my local train company. I am familiar because I learned how to ride a bicycle as a child, I eat Chinese food regularly enough to have become proficient with chopsticks, I use a keyboard everyday, and have travelled on trains frequently. I am familiar with these different forms of technology because I have to use them and because I have chosen to use them, and have watched other people use them, both in the real world and in a wide variety of media. I am able to demonstrate my familiarity with these diverse technologies not by having complex, abstract cognitive structures in my head (though they may well be in there somewhere) but demonstrating this *know-how* and comporting myself appropriately.

2.3.1 MAKING USE OF THE TACIT

So, if we cannot articulate familiarity, what possible use might it have? One very simple example is in the design of the first ever desktop graphical user interface (GUI) which can be found as part of the Xerox 8010 Information System (the Xerox "Star"). The GUI was described as follows: "Every user's initial view of Star is the Desktop, which resembles the top of an office desk, together with surrounding furniture and equipment. It represents a working environment, which current projects and accessible resources reside. On the screen are displayed pictures of familiar office objects, such

---

[1] Interestingly, although scripts, frames, and schemata may no longer have the currency they once did in AI, they continue to thrive in a variety of forms not least as the basis of scenario- and persona-based design within HCI.

as document folders, file drawers, in-baskets and out-baskets" (Smith, 1985). The guiding design philosophy for this user interface was to reproduce familiar elements of the office environment—folders filled with papers, a waste basket, a rolodex and so forth. Specifically, "There should be an explicit user's model of the system, and it should be familiar (drawing on objects and activities the user already works with) and consistent." This approach very clearly foregrounds the use of familiar features—such as folders, a desktop and so on to which its intended users brought their "know-how." In the real world of the late 1970s (prior to the advent of the paper-less office) people stored papers in folders and folders were kept in file drawers; new papers resided in in-trays and completed work was placed in the out basket. Knowing how to deal with this in the real world offered the opportunity to apply this *know-how* to the digital world without need for intervening metaphorical or analogical reasoning. (Thus the claim that this is in some sense metaphorical is a little misleading.)

A second example of familiarity can be found in any of the current generation of "smart phones" and tablet computers. Interaction with these devices relies on our ability to swipe, pinch, tap and so forth. These actions are so very familiar to us in the everyday world that we can readily cope with their novel implementation as a glass surface.

2.3.2 A STRUCTURE FOR PRIOR KNOWLEDGE

Blackler and her colleagues have reported studies of "technology familiarity" which they found to be good predictors of subsequent performance with new but similar or related products. They found that familiarity with products similar to the ones used in their studies resulted in their faster uptake. People with good "technology familiarity" began to use the new technology more quickly and used more of its features than those with poorer technology familiarity (Blackler et al., 2003a, 2003b). These observations have been echoed by Dixon and O'Reilly (2002) who have also argued that people almost never learn completely new procedures as they simply adapted their behaviour from prior knowledge. Blackler and Hurtienne (2007) have gone on to consider the role and structure of prior knowledge per se in the use of digital technology. They begin by re-iterating that the "use of products involves utilising knowledge gained through other experience(s). Therefore, products that people use intuitively are those with features they have encountered before." In making this observation they raise the issue of intuitiveness. Hurtienne and Israel (2007) describe a technical system as being intuitively usable if, "the users' unconscious application of pre-existing knowledge leads to effective interaction" (p. 128). This said, they have proposed a continuum or simple hierarchy of prior knowledge which underpins this intuitive use. This hierarchy is depicted in Figure 2.1.

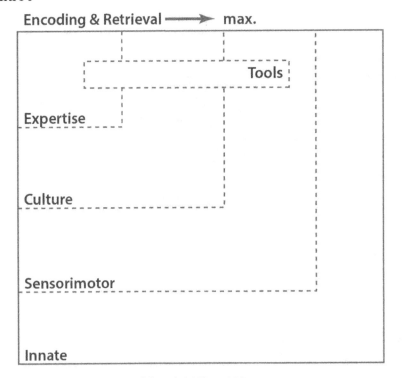

Figure 2.1: Re-drawn after Hurtienne and Israel, 2007 p. 128.

At the lowest level of this nested structure lies what the authors call *innate* knowledge which is the product of the prenatal stage of development. In keeping with developmental psychology, this kind of knowledge is said to be limited to reflexes and other instinctive behaviours. The next level is *sensorimotor* knowledge. This is they describe as "general knowledge" acquired during early childhood but which is subsequently used in our interactions with the world. Examples of this kind of knowledge include our ability to differentiate faces, the behaviour of the physical world including gravity and concepts such as speed and *image schemata*. Image schemata are a form of knowledge that represents very basic and repeated sensorimotor experiences. For example, the repeated experience of vertically arranged objects and of gravity forms the image schema UP-DOWN. Other examples of image schemata include CONTAINER, NEAR-FAR, and PATH among many more (Lakoff and Johnson, 1999). Image schemata have proved popular with theorists and practitioners in the field of tangible computing and the concept allows us to recognise that prior knowledge is not merely embedded ("in the head") but is embodied too ("in the body").

The next level of knowledge is described as being specific to the *culture* an individual lives in. Understandably the authors have not elaborated on this.

Finally, the most specific level of knowledge is that of *expertise*, that is, the kind of knowledge a doctor, mechanic, gamer, or academic might have. The knowledge we have about tools cuts across these boundaries of sensorimotor, culture, and expertise knowledge. At the sensorimotor level is the "know-how" associated with physically handling tools. At the culture level we find tools widely used by society such as mobile phones. In the highest stage there is the knowledge acquired from using tools in one's area of expertise, e.g., a mass spectrometer.

These different kinds of knowledge are also readily observable (more mundanely) by anyone who has used any of the current generation of gaming systems, such as the Sony EyeToy™, the Nintendo Wii™, or the Microsoft Kinect™. These technologies invite us to gesture, swipe, wave, smile, kick, and simulate the use of real and imaginary devices and weapons ranging from golf clubs and "light-sabres." In doing so we can witness sensorimotor behaviour, cultural knowledge (e.g., "just which end of a light sabre should I hold?"), and game playing expertise in action. However, the world is rarely this neatly organised.

2.3.3   COLLAGES AND VICARIOUS LEARNING

Our familiarity with digital technology is not merely the product of direct personal use as some of our experiences are vicarious. As a consequence we may find ourselves copying or mirroring others given our predisposition to imitate (e.g., Rizzolatti and Sinigaglia, 2006/2008). Tomasello (1999) observes that all primates can be viewed as selectively engaging the environment in a dyadic fashion, that is, establishing a contingent relationship between self and an environmental object but humans are also capable of creating triadic relationships. These triadic relationships comprise the self, another person, and what the other person is engaged with. In this way we learn about the properties of technology through another person's actions. We see examples of technology being used by others, in TV programmes, magazines, Web pages, and advertisements in a variety of media. A consequence of this is that our familiarity comprises an unstructured, serendipitous mixture of *know-how*, and scraps of propositional knowledge, heuristics, and even fragments of "magical thinking" and mental models. It is also fair to suggest that it may also contain misunderstandings and misapprehensions too. We borrow Tversky's term "cognitive collage" to capture this heterogeneity. She defines a cognitive collage (1993) as, "thematic overlays of multi-media from different points of view. They lack the coherence of maps (she is writing in the context of way-finding), but do contain figures, partial information, and differing perspectives." It may be that familiarity relies on a collage of prior knowledge rather than a neatly stacked hierarchy.

A moment of personal reflection offers some support for this lack of coherence. I have never swung a baseball bat, but I am confident that I could do so both in the real world and in a baseball (video) game. This because I have seen real baseball bats (in a sports store), seen them swung in U.S. movies and in at least one episode of Star Trek. I also know that baseball shares similarities with the English game "rounders" (and indeed there is evidence that the game may have been invented here in England) and I have a broad prior knowledge of bat and ball games. These experiences have resulted in my familiarity with baseball and with this a readiness to cope with a baseball bat while never having held one for real.

2.4   OUR INVOLVEMENT WITH DIGITAL TECHNOLOGY

Having defined familiarity with digital technology as the *readiness to cope* with it and being the product of repeated exposure to it (prior knowledge), we turn to its other aspect, namely that of *involvement*.

Heidegger (1971, p. 4) does, of course, warn us about confining our understanding of technology to the purely instrumental: "we shall never experience our relationship to the essence of technology so long as we merely conceive and push forward the technological [...] Everywhere we remain unfree and chained to technology, whether we passionately affirm or deny it. But we are delivered over to it in the worst possible way when we regard it as something neutral; for this conception of it, to which today we particularly like to do homage, makes us utterly blind to the essence of technology." Familiarity as a form of knowledge (for it surely is), is neither detached nor disinterested, as it is the consequence of being involved with, in this instance, digital technology. To be involved means to be "rolled up in", or enfolded or entangled. Thus to be involved with technology is to be rolled up in it or enfolded by it.

Having introduced a quotation from Heidegger, we do need to say a little about his work to develop this discussion further. Heidegger's language can be obscure for the specialist and non-specialist reader alike and as he (unhelpfully) put it himself, "Making itself intelligible is suicide for philosophy" (Wrathall, 2005). However, just as Descartes famously concluded that the only thing of which he could be certain was that he was thinking (the famous *cogito ergo sum*), Heidegger's starting premise is that we are in the world. This is more usually written as a hyphenated expression being-in-the-world, the hyphens reputedly indicating that nothing stands between us and the world. The world, of course, is not to be understood as planet Earth but as the artefactual, "man-made" world of technology. For Heidegger the world comprises a "web of significance" or "context of equipment" in which all human activity is located. We can then see that being in-the-world and rolled up in it are describing much the same experience, but what is the nature of involvement? We are involved with the world in the sense we cannot escape it. There is nowhere to go and nothing mediates our experience of it (remember the hyphens), as we have already seen our understanding of technology is not a matter of disinterested facts and figures but practical knowledge or "know-how."

Being involved with technology, we encounter it not as individual, separate tools but as an inter-related network of technology that we can use or as Heidegger would put it is "available" (ready-to-hand). Our involvement with the world is what opens up (discloses) the opportunities which technology offers us, so having encountered technology as available we also recognise that it can be used in-order-to achieve our ends by the application of our "know-how"—involvement and understanding working in concert. Heidegger tells us that "Equipment is essentially something in-order-to" and an in-order-to is a pretty good description of an affordance (Gibson, 1986) so when we make use of an in-order-to, it is equivalent to a engaging with a task (or exploiting an affordance). Tasks, in turn, need to be considered against the background of purpose and reason. Here we find another of Heidegger's hyphenated expressions for-the-sake-of something or other as he describes purpose (e.g., the reason we are using the technology). In short, we encounter technology as available, that is, offering possibilities for use (in-order-to's) that we exploit for-the-sake-of the activities we need to complete. Our relationship with technology does not end here as it also serves to define who we are. Heidegger regards who we are as being indeterminate and contingent, describing human beings as Dasein (a term which is usually left untranslated; Heidegger's Obscure Terminology). Dasein is grounded in what we do and in the tools we use, as these change so does our identity—from husband, to teacher, to cricket fan, to colleague—and as such allows us to equate people with their *know-how*. So, for example, a surgeon is defined in terms of their skills, that is, they are someone who knows-how to conduct surgery. In these terms, understanding digital technology means being able to use it skilfully, that is, demonstrating our familiarity with it (e.g., by making a phone call, navigating a website and so forth). In using these concepts we rephrase the discussion from human-computer interaction per se to how we encounter, cope with, and the means by which we create our identities.

2.5   NOT BEING FAMILIAR

This section draws upon our earlier published work in this area (e.g., Turner and Van De Walle, 2006; Turner et al., 2007) specifically, an extended study of a group of seniors in their residential home ("Redhouse") over a period of 10 months. This study was part of an initiative supported by the charity Age Concern Edinburgh, to provide an opportunity for a group of older people "to familiarize themselves with computers." Forty people registered for "lessons" thus forming the *Redhouse Computer Club*. None had ever used a computer before.

Of the forty computer club members, twenty volunteered to take part in this research (they are subsequently identified by their initials). We should note that the seniors themselves were all well educated, former professionals (including medical practitioners and lawyers) who proved to be thoughtful and insightful participants in this study. The experiences of this group were elicited by way of individual and group interviews and discussions lasting up to 90 min. The recorded interviews and discussions run to seventy hours and more than 25,0000 words after being transcribed (the empirical work was carried out by Van De Walle). As in much qualitative research, the process was fundamentally interpretive: meaning is often implicit and can only be understood through immersion with the entirety of the data. The major themes were identified as: Reconfiguring One's World, Computers are Part of Modern Life, Participating in the Modern World, and The Meeting of Two Worlds. These themes offer an insight into the nature of familiarity-unfamiliarity for this group.

2.5.1 RECONFIGURING ONE'S WORLD

For these participants, familiarising themselves with digital technology required the reconfiguration of their everyday lives. This process involved changes to their relationships, language, ownership, and perceptions. This section examines some of these changes.

SC (the initials of one of our participants) indicated that, "there are quite a lot of reasons for learning about computers, which really have nothing to do with the use of computers", one of which concerned computer terminology itself. Many of participants observed that "computer language" had now become part of everyday language. DM told us, "I am thinking about everyday language—sometimes people use the expression 'download', for example. Well, if you don't know anything about computers, you don't have a clue what that means." The presence of "computer language" in everyday language implies that it has penetrated the participants' everyday lives. They also noted that, as keen TV watchers, television programmes frequently show computers being used with numerous references to "websites" and email addresses. Another example of this change in everyday language was identified by SC who indicated that computing terms frequently appear in crossword clues. This, she believed, is a relatively recent phenomenon. According to her, this is not part of her generation's "knowledge." She revealed that her main motivation for learning to use computers was to upgrade her linguistic skills: "The only need that I have at the moment is not for the computer but the computer vocabulary because I am addicted to crosswords and for the last... just recently, they have started putting computer words in the answers to clues. That's really the only need I have for a computer at the moment."

2.5.2 COMPUTERS ARE PART OF 'MODERN LIFE'

Participants noted that computers have become so ubiquitous that they were actively defining modern living, JC observing that "everything is computerised now" and that "It's a part of modern life." She also mentioned the use of computers for library catalogues while other participants (e.g., SC, NS, NM) commented that computers are now used by doctors for consultations as well as by staff in hospitals and in banks. Consequently people have to be computer literate in order to be employable, and many people were retiring from work in preference to having to learn about computers.

2.5.3 PARTICIPATING IN THE MODERN WORLD

As we have seen, these participants see computers as actively defining the way in which the modern world works. They believe that those people unfamiliar with the technology are unable to understand situations where computers are involved and are excluded from the opportunities that computers afford (e.g., information retrieval, communication, saving money on shopping and so forth). DM, "... I do not share the hostility to computers, which I find in the opinions voiced by some of my friends, friends of my own age I may say. My own attitude is that the computer won't go away however hostile one may be to it and therefore it seems sensible to accept this fact and at least make an attempt to cope with what has become such an ever present part of modern life." DG, "I think that we are learning to fit in the world that is developing."

Younger people are seen to use computers, know about them, and speak the "computer language." DW and MT both believed that if they (the Redhouse group) were to acquire this "know-how" it would create a "link" between them and the current generation. This was seen to be important because most participants had direct relationships with younger people through their families.

MK argued that the modern world is putting pressure on her to take part in it. She indicated that the new technological world was affecting many of her everyday experiences. Eventually, everybody will have to be either part of it or "excluded from life." She argued that computers constitute something basic in the context of the modern ways of living, "The world is there. The world in which I have to function everyday is there and I am in it. And these machines are now in it. And I've got to come to terms with these machines if I am going to continue to live in this world." I'm sure Heidegger would be proud of MK.

2.5.4   THE MEETING OF TWO WORLDS

These seniors all acknowledged the existence of a new, unfamiliar, technological world. DW talked of a "technological age", MK of a "technological world", IB and MK of an "electronic world." MK stressed that a new world has emerged and that it extends far beyond the sphere of computers and technology, affecting virtually every aspect of life. MK said, "… I am standing at a point where I see a new world in every aspect, as I say, whether it's sport or religion or politics, or cooking or the telly [television] or anything […] I am being dragged, kicking and screaming into the new world by my family, who started me off on the movement out of the old world a long time ago. And in that respect I think that I am better placed than most to make the transition."

Participants indicated that they did not belong to this modern technological world. Contrasting the new and old the participants said that while the former involves mostly dealing with technology, the latter involves dealing with people. Beyond human relationships, IR also pointed to the predominance of language in his life, both oral and written. When she declared "there was nothing technical in my world" or "I haven't used that much in the way of technology", JC expressed a feeling common to many of the participants in noting that technology had only a peripheral role in their lives both at home and work (prior to retirement). Indeed these jobs had mostly involved other people or were done by hand. With such backgrounds, participants such as DW could say, "technology has not been part of my life." Echoing JC and DW, NS reported that she had "no experience whatever with technology" and that she sees it as "a completely new thing" to which she "hadn't paid much attention."

2.5.5 IN SUMMARY

These seniors saw familiarity with technology as a defining feature of modern life and that being fluent in "computer language" was essential if they were to function in the new, technologically defined world. By becoming familiar with technology it allowed them to be involved in the modern world whether it was in terms of online shopping, emailing relatives, or simply being able to solve a crossword puzzle.

2.6 FAMILIARITY WITHIN HCI

In the final section of this chapter we consider why and how familiarity appears in HCI research and reporting.

As already noted, familiarity is not a concept which has received sustained or very much direct attention within HCI. While a role for familiarity can be traced back to the very beginnings of the discipline, as we have seen, it was central to the design of the Xerox Star's user interface, it has, for whatever reasons, received scant attention and when it does appear it is never explicitly defined, rather being treated as a given. Bell et al. (2005) do offer an insight as to why this might be. They argue that there is a need to make *familiar* things *unfamiliar* so as to open their "design space." Their argument, it is hoped, is now a familiar one. Their interest is in the design of domestic technologies. They begin that, "Everyone is an expert on the home. Since our births, we have been immersed in, moved through, and made homes for ourselves. Across a range of locations and cultures, we have been bombarded with popular media imaginings of daily life and its literal and metaphorical trappings." They continue that as the home is a store of personal, cultural and so forth experiences, these assumptions are all too easily embedded in the design of domestic technology which, in turn, would serve to constrain design space itself. Hence the need for *de-familiarisation* to create a space for critical reflection. The authors note that the notion of de-familiarisation is a literary one and cite the work of Tolstoy and Lewis. They also note the use of the concept in anthropology, for example, Westerners' alienation from their own bodies. Perhaps familiarity is a little too *close* for many researchers to adopt a scientific or even a fresh perspective. Perhaps familiarity does indeed breed contempt, that is, something that can be disregarded. However, what follows is a selected review of how and where familiarity appears in the HCI literature. It will be seen that familiarity has been found be a factor in: (i) making sense of a task; (ii) the creation of shared meaning and appropriation; and (iii) achieving over-learning/automaticity. Considering examples of these in turn:

2.6.1 MAKING SENSE OF TASKS

Lim et al., (1996), using Action Identification Theory, found that familiarity with a given task was an important factor in how people construed that task. Action Identification Theory is a set of propositions that characterise the factors that influence how we think about events. These factors typically include notions of goal, purpose, implications and so forth. Lim and his colleagues used this framework as a means of understanding why direct manipulation is a successful interaction style. They found that highly familiar tasks are identified in terms of what needs to be done while less-familiar tasks focus on the means by which the task is to be accomplished. Action identification theory is itself based on the treatment of attention from the perspective of automaticity, that is, the extent to which tasks become automatic with increased familiarity.

In a related vein, Espinosa and Mares (2012) investigated the role familiarity plays in a player determining how suitable a challenge is within a game. In order for a player to experience *flow*, a balance must be struck between the player's skill levels and the challenges that he or she encounters. The researcher found that players were best able to judge the appropriateness of the challenge (or task as above) as a consequence of their familiarity with games.

Finally, and a little obliquely, familiarity (e.g., Freeman et al., 2000) also appears as a content factor in presence research. Presence, thinking or feeling oneself present in a virtual environment, is treated as a multi-factorial experience and familiarity with the (virtual) medium being one such factor. The degree to which one is familiar with the medium or substance of the virtual environment the greater the experience of presence. These findings have been echoed by Qin et al. (2009) who have demonstrated that familiarity with the game story significantly influences the players' experience of immersion.

2.6.2   SHARED MEANING

Familiarity has also been both proposed and used as the explicit basis of design. Here the distinction must be made between those approaches to design that argue for the use of metaphor and those which seek to use prior, real world knowledge and skills. Examples of this latter approach include: Mackay et al. (1998) who describe an augmented reality prototype designed to support air traffic controllers and their interactions with paper flight strips. By adopting an AR approach they sought to avoid the problem of "forcing an abrupt change in the controllers' familiar styles of interaction." Similarly Kasabach et al. (1998) have reported the development of digital ink that combines the familiar (everyone uses a pen) and the new (digital media). Digital Ink is described as a writing tool that "both understands people's handwriting, and allows them to turn any writing surface into a personalized interaction surface."

More recently a number of researchers have begun to see a place for familiarity in the design of tangible systems. Stößel (2009) found that older users were both faster and more accurate when they traced familiar gestures (such as ✓ and ✗) on a screen as opposed to unfamiliar gestures. Höök (2006) has proposed that familiarity may offer a solution to the issue of designing for appropriation. She draws upon examples from the participatory design of interactive surfaces. This approach empowers one group but raised the issue of how can the technology be designed in such a way that it can be open for interpretation by others and reflect longitudinal usage and the changes that brings.

Her solution is to build upon "what is familiar to people in their everyday communication practices with others and everyday physical, bodily encounters with the world" (p. 242). She continues, that these open surfaces have to be designed so that they reflect the users' own interpretation and to do that they must be familiar: reflecting with their real world practice, *know-how,* and prior knowledge. Finally, Herstad and Holone (2012) describe familiarity as an intimate understanding and engagement with the technology and, as such, is an excellent candidate for understanding and developing tangible interaction. Their theoretical position, like the current discussion, also draws on the work of Heidegger, Dreyfus, Lakoff, and Johnson.

2.6.3   LEARNING TO BE FAMILIAR

Manuals are another means by which people learn to use an interactive system, though they are conspicuously absent from the current generation of digital technology. Manuals are presented as the means by which we can acquire the necessary familiarity to get started, get the best out of the system and diagnose problems. Although many will specifically state "no prior knowledge required" this, of course, cannot be so as all new knowledge is built upon our familiarity with the world. At one extreme, manuals are a means of achieving automaticity, an example of which is the NASA Project Gemini Familiarization Manual (McDonnell Corporation, 1965). This manual is a description of the spacecraft's systems and "The manual is intended as a familiarization-indoctrination aid and as a ready reference for detailed information on a specific system or component." Indoctrination, which is more usually associated with all encompassing teachings and belief, conveys the practice of "over-learning" by which the astronauts became "one" with their spacecraft.

Finally, familiarity has an underexplored affective component too. For example, why does it feel so good to get home after a long day or to sleep in our own bed rather than in an hotel room? We know of this dimension by way of (irresistible) anecdote and maxim in that we are warned, as we have already seen, that familiarity breeds contempt and children (attributed to Mark Twain). Titchner (1928, p. 408) more prosaically reported that in a study of recognition that his subjects reported glow of warmth, a sense of ownership, a feeling of intimacy, a sense of being at home, a feeling of ease, or a comfortable feeling.

2.7   IN SUMMARY

Familiarity has an overlooked, taken-for-granted quality about it. Yet if the world were not familiar we would be faced with the untenable problem of learning afresh each day. We would not survive being unable to dress or feed ourselves, while updating our profiles on our favourite social media sites would remain an unarticulated mystery. Despite being largely unremarked, familiarity was there guiding the development of the first GUI and continues to have a rarely articulated role in the design of contemporary digital technology. From this reading, familiarity has a meme-like quality. A meme (Dawkins, 1976) is something like "a unit of culture" which is passed from one individual to another by means of imitation or simple proximity and which conveys an advantage of some kind. Our familiarity with digital technology may be a product of this kind of transmission and does, for many, offer an advantage (though quantifying that advantage presents something of a challenge) (Familiarity as a Meme).

Familiarity as a Meme

Dawkins (**1976**) coined the term meme in an effort to capture the idea of "cultural transmission" operating in a manner analogous to the biological. While the gene is the fundamental unit of biological (information) transmission and with it, the ability to replicate, the *meme* is the equivalent "unit of culture", transmitted from one to another, replicating as it goes and offering some kind of advantage to the receiver. It has been suggested that memes operate like a virus, spreading ideas as diverse as religion and racism, but there is yet to be a convincing, critical discussion of how they might work.

Here I suggest that the work of Ilyenkov, which many regard as being wilfully obscure (even more so than Heidegger), may actually provide a mechanism. Elsewhere I have used a similar argument to offer a social perspective on the nature of affordance (**Turner, 2005**). The following description of Ilyenkov's work draws on Bakhurst's lucid commentary (**1991**) on this most challenging of philosophers.

In accounting for the pervasiveness of familiarity Ilyenkov's argument might run something like this: we can identify two classes of nonmaterial phenomena, namely: (i) mental phenomena such as thoughts, beliefs, and feelings and (ii) phenomena that are neither material nor mental—meaning and values, such as *goodness*.

This second class he calls *ideal*, which in turn can be considered in two ways. An objectivist account might argue that such ideal phenomena are external to us and constrain our actions, while a subjectivist account would argue that these phenomena are the product of our human nature and as such are merely projections and have no existence independent of us. Rejecting both of these accounts Ilyenkov proposes a position arguing that a thing can be objective without being independent of us.

By way of example, Ilyenkov (**1977**) describes how ideal properties can be enscribed and exist objectively in the world. He uses the example of a table. A table is part of objective reality and yet can be distinguished from a block of wood because it has been objectified by the human activity shaping it. This is how we distinguish wood from tables. Wood affords a variety of uses, for example, burning, throwing, shaping, trading, and so forth. Through these purposive uses, objects acquire significance. Ilyenkov notes that activity is the source of the world we inhabit and the principal expression of how we inhabit it. This is more than saying simply that objectification is the source of the ideal properties of this or that thing—Ilyenkov was proposing that objectification is the source of human culture. So, for example, we non-archaeologists are unable to distinguish between a shard of flint and an ancient stone tool while a student of the discipline who has been successfully encultured can. Ideality is like a stamp or inscription on the substance of nature by social human activity. A significance makes a thing knowable. For Ilyenkov, nothing about the physical nature of a thing in itself explains how it is possible that it can be knowable. The ideal properties of an artefact represent the reification or embodiment of the practices of the human community that has historically developed the thing. In other words, objects acquire this ideal content not as the result of being accessed by an individual mind, but by the historically developing activities of communities of practice.

Through human activity we idealise our world (i.e., endow it with meaning) and in so doing we also endow it with properties that come to exist completely independently of us. Ideal properties are thus real, objective but not independent of us as they are products of meaning-endowing in human activity. Familiarity is potentially such an ideal property.

However, the most problematic part of this argument is the issue of ideality's complete independence from the individual mind. The key to understanding this is the expression "individual mind" rather than minds per se. Thus the ideal exists in the collective not the individual mind. Thus while life is a product of the collective, it is experienced by individuals as a set of given rules, practices, tools, and artefacts. We, individually, grow up among pre-existing and apparently objective phenomena. From this perspective human development can be seen as the process of becoming en-culturated into this objectified, historically developed world. For being en-cultured, we can read "familiar."

We began this chapter by adopting Heidegger's treatment of familiarity that claimed that it comprised involvement and understanding. Involvement is what underpins our use, interest in, and engagement with technology. Our involvement is what makes us interact with it by disclosing what it can do for us. Understanding technology is the "know-how" which readies us to cope with it.

Having discussed familiarity we are now ready to cope.

Rewritable Routines

Baber and Stanton (**1997**) have described an approach to human-product interaction called "rewritable routines" which is of interest to the current discussion. They begin by noting that physical appearance of a tool, digital or otherwise, presents information to the potential user in a variety of formats. This they describe as the "system image." Some aspects of this image are persistent (e.g., the physical appearance) while other aspects emerge as a consequence of interaction or use. They propose that the system image *implies* (affords) a set of routines (sequences or patterns of behaviour) that the person can employ, and that the selected routine will depend on the user's goal, prior experience, and their familiarity with the product (tool or technology). These *rewritable routines* may be thought of as user-defined scripts which develop and are adapted dynamically as an interaction progresses. Their "re-writability" refers to the fact that they are susceptible to contingent change ranging from minor amendments to being completely overwritten.

In all, once understood, the tool "affords" and guides a possible set of actions. They tell us that if the goal, and the form and function, of the technology correspond then the interaction will be intuitive, examples of which may be found in the ergonomics literature where it is known as "S–R compatibility." The work of Murrell offers many such examples including the design of physical knobs and dials for which "up" means "more" and "down" means "less." Similarly, rotating a knob clockwise affords increasing the volume or the amount, likewise an anticlockwise direction signifies a lessening or reduction (**Murrell, 1965**). Baber and Stanton describe these kinds of routines as "stereotypes", and for the user it is simply a matter of matching the system image with a stereotyped response. In considering rewritable routines, it is very difficult not to be struck by similarity of these S–R compatibilities with Lakoff and Johnson's image schemata.

CHAPTER 3

Coping

3.1 KEY POINTS

- Coping means "absorbed engagement" and is a term that philosophers have used to describe our everyday dealings with the world. Our ability to drive a car, write our name, play a sport, and a thousand other everyday things are examples of coping. In this chapter, the definition of coping focused on our absorbed engagement with digital technology.

- Philosophically, coping has been described in a number of distinct but related ways but all accounts agree that it primarily stands in contrast to *detached deliberation*. We do not have to stop and think or have to plan when we are engaged in familiar activities. There is a place for deliberation but this tends to be confined to when we encounter something unfamiliar, or when things go wrong, or when we are engaged in "deep thought."

- Coping does not rely on a mental or cognitive representation of the world, the task or the technology being used to achieve one's goal.

- Coping is embodied, that is, our corporality plays a central role in integrating and mediating our engagement with the world. Embodiment may be the most important but is almost certainly the least well understood aspect of coping.

- From a psychological perspective, coping may be thought of as "intuitive thinking in action." It is quick, effective, and frequently automatic.

- We are able to cope with digital technology because we are familiar with it and have the necessary "know-how" to use it effectively.

- Finally, coping does not refer to solicitude, that is, it is not about getting over a setback or loss.

3.2 INTRODUCTION

Having proposed in the introduction to this lecture that our dealing with technology may be characterised as "coping", this chapter outlines three different philosophical accounts of it.

Etymologically to *cope* means to vie with, to match, to strike, to encounter (Skeat, 1879) and it is from this perspective of active engagement that we now consider these similar but distinct accounts of coping. These accounts are descriptions of our *absorbed engagement* with our everyday worlds of work, travel, leisure—not just digital technology.

The origins of these philosophical accounts are varied. Hubert Dreyfus' *practical coping* brings together his work on making sense of Heidegger's profound and complex writings with his own continuing criticisms of Artificial Intelligence research.

The second account is drawn from the writings of Francisco Valera. Valera's work stems from a biological perspective with a sprinkling of Tibetan Buddhism. His interests included the self-organisation of organisms and other complex systems while collaboration with Thompson and Rosch led to the publication of *The Embodied Mind: Cognitive Science and Human Experience* (1991), which formed the basis and inspiration for the subsequent work on enactive interaction.

Finally, Michael Wheeler is, in many respects, the most contemporary of these writers, as he treats coping from a position of "online" intelligence which is designed ("has evolved") to deal with the world. Although explicitly philosophical, Wheeler writes with an eye to cognitive science and a little Harry Potter (sic).

It is also recognised that coping is an expression of our embodiment and while all three of the above accounts make some claim to embodiment, the literature on embodiment is briefly introduced.

Of the accounts, without doubt Dreyfus' exposition is the best developed and most detailed. Rouse, writing of Dreyfus' work, suggests that his greatest contribution has been this "phenomenological articulation of embodied, practical coping" (Rouse, 2000, p. 7). Valera differs from the Heidegger/Dreyfus position in that he identifies the source of immediate coping in the repeated sensorimotor experiences we have with our bodies in the particular situations. Like practical coping, immediate coping does not rely on an underlying representation. Wheeler's position is to observe that smooth coping has been "designed" for dealing with real world, real time situations and, as such, also operates without an underlying representation. Ultimately the Dreyfus position is quite radical, writing that, "Heidegger's crucial insight is that being-in-the-world is more basic than thinking and solving problems; it is not representational at all. That is, when we are coping at our best, we are drawn in by solicitations and respond directly to them, so that the distinction between us and our equipment vanishes" (Dreyfus, 2007, p. 254).

We conclude this chapter with a discussion of coping and its relationship to intuitive behaviour.

3.3   PRACTICAL COPING

Dreyfus was the first to articulate a neo-Heideggerian account of coping, which he defines as, "the mostly smooth and unobtrusive responsiveness to circumstances that enable human beings to get around in the world." This quotation, in many ways, captures the genesis of this lecture. The question it raised was, if we cope successfully with the complexity of the modern world, is digital technology excluded from this smooth and unobtrusive responsiveness?

Dreyfus variously prefixes *coping* with the words practical, engaged, and embodied but for the purposes of this discussion we adopt *practical coping*. Practical coping is the skilful and representation-free dealing with the world. It comprises the repertoire of background skills upon which we rely and as such includes the full range of our productive, everyday habits and routines.

Practical coping is at work when we eat a meal, write our monthly reports, make a phone call, play a game of cricket, surf the Web, and use all manner of tools. It extends beyond the mundane to include the expert performances of the skilled athlete, the surgeon, and chess master (Dispensing with Representation). As you are reading this, you are coping. If you are reading the physical text, you are coping by skilfully holding the volume, by reading the words, and by turning the pages as required.

Dispensing with Representation: Becoming Expert

Perhaps one of the most frequently quoted examples of Dreyfus' work is his account of becoming expert which he created with his brother (**Dreyfus and Dreyfus, 1980**). It is of interest here because of its specific emphasis on the non-representational nature of skilled "know-how." He asks us to imagine an individual learning to play chess, drive a car, or become a surgeon and identifies five stages in the acquisition of these skills. The first stage is the novice which is typified by the "rigid adherence to taught rules or plans" and the failure to exercise any kind of "discretionary judgment." This is, "pawns move one square forward unless it is the first time it has been moved"; or "mirror-signal-manoeuvre" for the learner driver.

The next stage is that of the advanced beginner who has acquired limited "situational perception" but still treats all aspects of work treated separately and with equal importance.

Acquiring more skill, we find those rare individuals who might be described as competent. People who are competent are able to cope with competing activities and an abundance of information. At this stage there is evidence of deliberate planning and the formulation and use of routines.

People who have acquired proficiency are said to have an holistic view of their environment; are able to prioritise; can detect patterns and deviation from the norm; and employ heuristics to deal with evolving situations.

Finally, expertise is based on transcending rules, guidelines, and heuristics as an expert has an "intuitive grasp of situations based on deep, tacit understanding." They are flexible and may have a vision of what might be. Thus expertise and its acquisition is about abandoning rules and formal structures, not their skilful manipulation.

Practical coping is directed at the world and comprises the following elements: firstly, practical coping is *comportment* (Chapter 2) rather than relying on the manipulation of cognitive structures and representations. There are no mental models or schemata in this account. Indeed, it is not possible, even in principle, to derive rules to capture the nature of practical coping as it is direct and unmediated. Comportment is our material responsiveness to the world.

Secondly, practical coping relies an adaptive repertoire of responses to the demands and opportunities offered by the world. It is not simply an example of a stimulus-response pairing as we respond flexibly and smoothly to situations unless we encounter a breakdown (more of which below). Practical coping is situated. It does not depend upon pre-formulated, conscious plans that we execute but is a description of our responsiveness to real world situations.

Finally, and this may surprise a little, practical coping is not directed at discrete things in the world because, as discussed in the last chapter, this account recognises that everything is interconnected. For example, you are not reading these words as a random, unconnected act. The practical coping with this text only makes sense in the broader context of, say, killing time at an airport, proof reading, or as academic endeavour. Thus practical coping is situated in a network of involvements. We read books at airports to kill time while we wait for our flight to a meeting; the manuscript is proofread to improve subsequent readability and to ensure that it conforms to the publisher's standards; we study academic texts to ensure that we stay up to date with our discipline. We read, we hammer, we use cutlery in order to achieve goals which, in turn, allow us to achieve our wider aims or purpose which, in turn, is located in a wide network of purposes (the "for-the-sake-of-whichs" of Chapter 2).

Having described some aspects of the structure of practical coping we now consider how is it experienced. As our focus is the use of digital technology we will confine this discussion to two aspects of this experience, namely, transparency and absorption.

The issue of transparency has been a matter of interest within HCI for many years and has been considered in a number of different forms: for example, successful interaction with digital technology "disappears" or becomes "transparent." So, in writing this, the computer I am using and this version of MS Word per se have disappeared into the background allowing me to concentrate on composing this text. Heidegger would have us believe that carpenters have much the same experience in hammering with the appropriate hammer. However for other researchers, it is the interaction itself that becomes "transparent" or "flows" and for still others, it is the individual who also becomes transparent—becoming lost or absorbed in the moment (e.g., Bødker, 1991; Dey et al., 2001; Streitz, 2008, among many others). All that is left is practical coping.

Artefacts tend to become transparent to the individual when he or she is fully engaged and absorbed with them. The engaged, absorbed individual is not aware of the technology as separate objects. This absorption also resembles the sense of flow described by Csikszentmihalyi (1990; 1992) (Why Coping Is Not Flow). As Heidegger puts it, "Self and world are not two entities, like subject and object." There is no separate individual, there is no separate world, there are no separate items of equipment (tools) there is only, "concerned absorption in the world." Indeed, more than this, Heidegger directly equates ourselves (Dasein) with absorption, "Dasein … is nothing but … concerned absorption in the world" (HCT, 197). If this sounds a little mystical, then it will come as no surprise to learn that Mahayana Buddhist linkages have been identified in Heidegger's work (May, 1996).

Why Coping Is Not Flow

Csikszentmihalyi's treatment of flow has some relevance here as it shares some of the properties of coping. The origins of flow lie with Csikszentmihalyi's observations of the creative process in artists. He found that when their work was going well they tended to disregard hunger, fatigue, and discomfort. Equally, however, they were found to rapidly lose interest when the work was completed. The question then was, "what motivated the artists to behave this way?." This phenomenon of intrinsic motivation Csikszentmihalyi named autotelic (literally, self goal). Having studied examples of intrinsic motivation in a variety of settings he found two common themes: (i) perceived challenge or opportunities for action that stretch existing skills; and (ii) clear proximal goals and immediate feedback. Csikszentmihalyi found similarities across work and play.

When experiencing flow, one is totally absorbed in the activity at hand. This is not dissimilar from being absorbed in, say, watching an action movie. However with flow the absorption is autotelic and is not the result of vicarious, passive engagement. When in flow the individual is said to operate at full capacity but flow is a matter of dynamic equilibrium being a balance between an individual's skills, capacities, and the opportunities offered. So, for example, if skills exceed opportunities, the individual experiences relaxation then boredom, while if challenges exceed skills then this results in anxiety. A given individual can find flow in almost any activity—working a cash register, ironing clothes, driving a car (p. 91)—and almost any pursuit—a museum visit, a round of golf, a round of chess—can bore or create anxiety. Donner and Cziksentmihalyi (**1992**) claim that employees experience flow 44% of the time at work, boredom 20%, and anxiety the remaining 36%. Sutton and his colleagues observed that Csikszentmihalyi's conception of flow requires a challenge, the sense of having one's skills constantly stretched: as he puts it, "although the flow experience appears to be effortless, it is far from being so", and often involves "highly disciplined mental activity" in the form of "complex mental operations … completed in a few seconds, perhaps in a fraction of a second." More simply we flow when the challenge is neither too difficult nor too simple and when our skills are appropriate, that is, neither over or underused.

Occasionally, of course, things go wrong and Dreyfus also offers an account of when this happens, identifying two kinds of disturbance. A disturbance occurs when there is either a temporary or total breakdown in our use of digital technology. These breakdowns shift us from being engaged in absorbed coping to foregrounding the breakdown itself. While Dreyfus offers a detailed analysis of the resulting experiences, these are not our focus here, as the intention of this lecture is to describe the ways in which we successfully cope with digital technology. It is recognised that coping is intrinsically difficult to study because it *just works* and it is far from clear how the researcher can, as it were, "lift a corner" to see how it operates (other than appealing to philosophy). Faced with such a problem we typically resort to examining where things fail or break down. A similar situation was encountered by researchers into visual perception in the 1960s. Like coping, visual perception just works. We find our way about the world with our apparently flawless visual perceptual system successfully processing the visual inputs. Researchers such as Richard Gregory, frustrated by this, hit upon the notion of studying visual ("optical") illusions as a means of "lifting the corner" on visual perception (Gregory, 1966; 1970). Though this particular form of breakdown analysis did offer insights into how the perceptual system worked it was limited to rather restricted, laboratory conditions. It did not result in an account of visual perception which is accepted today—which, instead is based on its usual operation. It is interesting to note in passing that it has been suggested that Gregory was motivated, at least in part, to create this strongly cognitivist account in response to Gibson's ecological approach which gave us direct perception and the concept of affordance, sentiments which are close to the spirit of our discussion.

3.4 IMMEDIATE COPING

Valera's *immediate coping* is a treatment of everyday cognition which is based on skilled behaviour. More formally, the origins of this form of coping can be traced back to the work discussed in Varela, Thompson and Rosch's book *The Embodied Mind*, which is an extended argument for the rejection of the traditional view of cognition with a view to replacing it with a form of embodied cognition. The authors characterise embodied cognition as arising from the experiences we have with our bodies—specifically those which are the result of our "recurrent patterns of sensorimotor capabilities", echoing the sentiments of Lakoff and Johnson, and that these capabilities are located in a broad biological, psychological, and cultural context (Valera et al., 1991, p. 173). This treatment of embodied cognition subsequently evolved into what became known as enactive cognition, of which, immediate coping itself is an expression. The clearest articulation of immediate coping appears in Valera's *Ethical Know-How* (1992). Ethical know-how is not concerned with abstract reasoning, as "the proper units of knowledge are primarily concrete, embodied, incorporated, lived; that knowledge is about situatedness; and that the uniqueness of knowledge, its historicity and context, is not a 'noise' concealing an abstract configuration in its true essence" (p. 7). Thus our immediate coping with situations, people, and technology is an expression of enactive cognition. Enactive accounts do not treat the world as a given—out there—but as, "something we engage in by moving, touching, breathing, and eating" (p. 8). From this position it follows that knowing-how is dependent upon those experiences we have in our own particular bodies with their particular sensorimotor capacities embedded in the particularities of the body's own biological being and cultural setting. Our know-how is personal.

Varela illustrates the difference between this kind of immediate coping and action, which is the-result-of-deliberation. He begins by contrasting Piaget's treatment of morality in children (this may seem a curious choice but Valera was writing about ethics at the time). Piaget argued that *pure reason* is "the arbiter both of theoretical reflection and daily practice" and that to understand judgment and behaviour one must understand the underlying cognitive processes, this *pure reason*. Valera is highly critical of this "reason-first" approach to behaviour arguing that the focus should be understanding the skilled behaviour itself and not the inferred context-free judgments upon which it is said to depend. Valera illustrates this neatly by considering our response to an old person having tripped and fallen in the street—do we immediately run to help or adopt a legal, medical or ethical position first and then act as a consequence of that deliberation? Most of us (excepting lawyers perhaps) simply act to help.

Immediate coping makes use of that which is available, proximal, and "handy", Varela arguing that "we always operate in some kind of immediacy of a given situation. Our lived world is so ready-at-hand that we have no deliberateness about what it is and how we inhabit it" (p. 9). Varela underlines the themes of acting without conscious deliberation in response to the demands and affordances of the situation. Immediate coping can also be thought of as *phronesis* (prudence), practical wisdom or even, and this term is not used without a certain amount of hesitation, "common sense."

Finally, Valera, in common with Dreyfus, recognises that everyday life is not consistently "smooth sailing" and that there are occasions when our various psychological systems let us down. In such situations we resort to deliberation to make sense of our situation and find a way back to the "transparent and stable."

3.5   SMOOTH COPING

Most recently, Wheeler (2005) has used the term *smooth coping* to designate "the sort of hitch-free skilled practical activity revealing of the ready-to-hand" (p. 129). Wheeler suggests the image of the skilled (motor car) driver effortlessly dealing with driving conditions and other traffic as an example of this. However, Wheeler writes that it would be wrong to equate smooth coping with mere patterns of coupled action-perception; instead, smooth coping is dynamic and flexible writing, "Our most direct and revealing relationship with equipment obtains when we display, through actual smooth coping, our knowledge of how to manipulate equipmental entities [such as digital technology] in appropriate ways" (p. 130).

Wheeler's position is to locate coping within an embodied-embedded paradigm which he describes as "putting cognition back in the brain, the brain back in the body and the body back in the world" (p. 11) which is the theme of his *Reconstructing the Cognitive World* (2005). This book, like Dreyfus before him, draws heavily on Heidegger to challenge many of the Cartesian assumptions that still lie at the heart of Artificial Intelligence (AI) and to some extent HCI. This embodied-embedded treatment in cognitive science is approximately equivalent to what we describe as "situated" in HCI terms. More than this, like Varela, this treatment of cognition is a primary kind of intelligence that has been "designed" for controlling action.

Wheeler distinguishes between what he describes as "online" intelligence, which involves the use of sensorimotor couplings and situated activity, and "offline" cognition, which is not concerned with coping with the current context.

He directly links Heidegger's concept of the ready-to-hand to this "online" intelligence: "A creature displays online intelligence just when it produces a suite of fluid and flexible real-time adaptive responses to incoming sensory stimuli" (p. 12). Thus smooth coping is fluid, real-time adaption in action. In contrast, "offline" intelligence is equated with experiencing the world as present-at-hand, that is, as in terms of detached, reflective deliberation (e.g., remembering your wife's birthday or the atomic weight of cobalt). Occupying the space "between" online and offline intelligence, Wheeler proposes un-readiness-to-hand (or unavailability). He observes (2004, p. 707, footnote 14) that no intelligent agent is ever wholly online or wholly offline, "On this view, intelligence is always a dynamic negotiation between on-line and off-line processes." And this negotiation lies with the body, as Whitehead has observed, "… the body is the organism whose states regulate our cognition of the world" (Whitehead, 1925, p. 91).

In summary, Wheeler relates these three forms of intelligence to corresponding forms of explanation.

He equates online intelligence with the kind of non-representational, embodied explanations which Dreyfus and Valera have presented. At the other extreme he relates offline intelligence with classical computational/representational explanatory approaches, and in the middle Wheeler calls for, "action-oriented representations" (Action-Oriented Representation).

Action-Oriented Representation

Clark has introduced the idea of representation being either "weak" and "strong" (e.g., **Clark, 1997a**; **1997b**; and **Clark and Grush, 1999**). A weak representation is an internal state that is capable of bearing information about an external object only when that object is in close proximity. Weak representations are found in what Clark describes as "information and control systems", which provide animals with quick feedback about objects in the immediate environment and thus enable them to interact with such local objects effectively. These systems contain internal states that are "information-bearing" in the sense that they correlate, in a non-accidental fashion, with features of external objects. If the source object of a weak representation becomes distal or absent, however, the representation becomes unavailable. However, such representations can be stored offline for future use.

A strong representation, in contrast, is an information-bearing state that is serviceable even if its source object becomes distal or absent. Clark argues that "a creature uses full-blooded internal representations if and only if it is possible to identify within the system specific states ... whose functional role is to act as de-coupleable surrogates for specifiable (usually extra-neural) states of affairs" (**Clark and Grush, 1999**, p. 8). According to Clark, if a system does not possess "the capacity to set-up and manipulate inner models instead of operating directly upon the world, it will fail to count as a locus of full-blooded internal representation" (**ibid**, p. 9). For Clark, strong representations count as genuine representations because agents actually use them as surrogates for other objects. Weak representations, in contrast, do not count as genuine representations, for while it may be convenient to describe these states as representational, agents themselves do not actually use them as representational surrogates. So, as Clark would have it, weak representations are active when the animal is engaged with its world (the world contributing to its own representation) while, correspondingly, strong representations are active when the animal is disengaged from the world.

How does this related to the use of digital technology? This is easily illustrated: imagine using an ATM, we can readily visualise the steps and simulate the behaviour of the system in our mind's eye. This is an example of strong representation perhaps as a mental model (e.g., **Payne, 1991**). Now contrast this with actually withdrawing some cash. This is achieved simply as part of our coping. The only recourse to deliberation is when we attempt to withdraw the cash without being mugged.

Having considered these philosophical perspectives on coping, what emerges is that they are all describing very similar experiences but one which sounds suspiciously like intuitive behaviour. Hold that thought.

3.6 EMBODIED COPING

Whether *embodied coping* merits separate consideration is moot as the three philosophical positions we have just considered all lay claim to being embodied accounts. The only remaining hurdle is to recognise that there is no account of embodied coping as such! As for research into embodied cognition the problem is more a matter of identifying which of the available accounts to consider. One of the earliest reviews of embodied cognition was by Wilson (2002) who described six variants;

a couple of years later Klemmer et al. (2006) favoured five accounts, while most recently, Shapiro (2011) settled on three. Interestingly though, Chemero (2009), in his *Radical Embodied Cognitive Science* has questioned the need for only one clear agreed account of embodiment, arguing that specific accounts are better able to explain specific behaviours. Indeed that might appear to be the case here.

Shapiro's three candidate accounts are based on the work of Valera, Thelen, and Clark respectively. The first two of these are a little too distant from the current discussion to be of immediate relevance. Of these Valera's work is the most radical and supposes that our experience of the world is actually the externalisation of our own sensorimotor systems. Thelen's work is based on dynamic systems theory and recognises a mutually shaping interaction among, the body, cognition, and the world. This leaves Clark's highly influential work which Shapiro neatly captures as "Thinking with the Body" (Thinking with Our Hands).

Of the considerable corpus of Clark's work, his extended mind hypothesis, which he developed with David Chalmers (1998), certainly seems the most useful here. This places cognition in the brain, body, and those aspects of the environment which might serve to solve the problems facing us, of which he writes, "whatever mix of problem-solving resources will yield an acceptable result with minimum effort" (Clark, 2008, p.13).

Attempting to find common ground among these three different accounts with specific reference to coping is no small matter. However, perhaps we can characterise the point of agreement as embodiment is the "moment-by-moment use of the space around us." This use of space is not an after thought but is integral to the ways in which we cope with the world. Now, back to that thought. Thank you for holding.

Thinking with Our Hands

While gesturing with our hands is usually treated as an adjunct to verbal communication, there are a very substantial number of studies which indicate that this is too narrow an understanding. So, do we think with our hands, or more specifically, just how does gesture help us cope with the world?

The literature on gesture is surprisingly diverse and multi-disciplinary and these few words can barely do it justice. However, that being said, gesture has been identified as a complementary strategy which is another way of saying epistemic action (**Kirsh, 1995b**) and as a means of lightening cognitive load (e.g., **Goldin-Meadow et al., 1991**, among very many others); as an example of simulated action (**Hostetter and Alibali, 2008**); and as part of our wider cognitive system (**Clark, 2008**).

Kirsh defines a complementary strategy as one which recruits external elements to reduce cognitive load and he includes examples of gesturing and thinking with our hands in this.

He suggests pointing, arranging the position and orientation of artefacts so as to simplify perception. He found that, for example, when people were asked to determine the dollar value of collections of coins placed before them they were slower and more error prone when they were not allowed to touch the coins or to move their hands.

Rauscher et al. (**1996**) also found that when people are prevented from gesturing when describing a spatial scene they showed significantly poorer fluency in their descriptions and those who were. These findings neatly making a lie of the old admonition (typically directed at children in toy stores), "look with your eyes not with your hands."

Goldin-Meadow and her colleagues have established a considerable body of work in this area and among their findings is evidence that gesturing lightens cognitive load for both adults and children; and that gesture is tightly linked to the development of spoken language. While Wang and Nass (**2005**) have reported studies which have demonstrated that physical mobility appears to be directly linked to increased creativity.

All this demonstrates the fundamentally embodied nature of many forms of epistemic action.

3.7 IS COPING SIMPLY INTUITIVE BEHAVIOUR?

Long before cognition was thought to be embedded, embodied, situated, distributed and so forth, it was treated as having only two modes, namely, *intuitive* or *inferential*. Indeed this is arguably the most fundamental distinction, and our descriptions of coping so far have sounded remarkably like *intuitive cognition* or perhaps *intuitive cognition in action*. To determine whether this observation has merit we now consider the nature of these two forms of cognition.

3.7.1 TWO MODES OF COGNITION

Thomson writes of this distinction as follows: "Intuition and Inference usually are contrasted with each other as being two separate and antithetical modes of mental experience. Intuition is generally referred to as primary and fundamental, while Inference is accounted secondary and superstructive […] Intuition has been regarded as a source of or method of obtaining transcendental, pure and trustworthy knowledge; while Inference has been esteemed to yield only experiential, mixed and uncertain information" (Thomson, 1878, p. 339 capitalisation in the original). Thus Thomson recognised the primacy of intuition as it is the most readily available and reliable form of cognition, with inferential cognition offering mixed and uncertain blessings.

From a more contemporary perspective, Riva and Mantovani (2012) have reviewed the differences between these two forms of cognition noting that while different authors may disagree on details, there is broad consensus. This agreement is summarised in Table 3.1.

Table 3.1: After Riva and Mantovani (2012)		
	Intuition	**Reasoning**
Process	relatively fast, parallel, automatic, cognitively effortless, associative, acquisition by biology, exposure, and personal experience	relatively slow, serial, controlled, cognitively effortful, rule-based acquisition by cultural and formal tuition
Content	percepts, imagery, and motor representations	conceptual / linguistic representations
Outcomes	impressions	judgments

Intuitive cognition is deemed to be fast, automatic, and involuntary while inferential cognition is slower and deliberate. Inferential cognition may also be described, in more familiar terms, as reasoning or deliberation while intuition is more perception-like, that is, seamless, immediate, and unmediated. Again from what we have described so far, coping does indeed share many of the characteristics of intuition.

Kahneman (2002; 2011, among many others) offers his own treatment of this distinction with particular reference to how we make judgments. Most recently, he distinguishes between what he describes as System 1 and System 2 thinking or, more snappily, as Fast Thinking, Slow Thinking in a book of the same name (2011). System 1 thinking operates, "automatically and quickly, with little or no effort and no sense of voluntary control" (p. 20). He contrasts this with System 2 thinking which, "allocates attention to the effortful mental activities that demand it, including complex computations. The operations of System 2 being associated with the subjective experience of agency, choice, and concentration" (p. 21). By way of illustration, he offers the following examples (Table 3.2) of both System 1 and System 2 activities in what he describes as a "rough order" of complexity:

Table 3.2: Adapted from Kahneman (2011, pages 21 & 22)	
System 1 thinking	**System 2 thinking**
detect that one object is more distant than another	brace for the starter gun in a race
complete the phrase "bread and ..."	search memory to identify a surprising sound
answer the question 2+2 = ?	recalling and telling someone your telephone number
read words on large billboards	compare two washing machines for overall value
understand simple sentences	fill out a tax form

More formally, Kahneman (2002) illustrates the components of these two systems. As can be seen from Figure 3.1, the perceptual system and the intuitive operations of System 1 generate involuntary impressions of the attributes of objects of perception and thought. The label "intuitive" is applied to those judgments which arise directly from impressions. In contrast, System 2 is involved in all judgments, whether they originate in impressions or from deliberate reasoning.

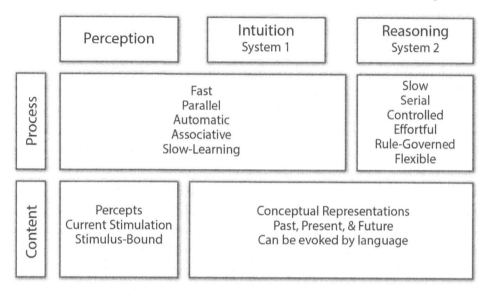

Figure 3.1: Re-drawn from an unlabelled figure in Kahneman, 2002, p. 451.

Although Kahneman separates perception and intuition in this model, a point with which not all authors agree, he nonetheless identifies a defining property of intuitive thought: they come to mind spontaneously—just like percepts.

Finally, intuition also suggests the affective or visceral ("gut feeling"), Westcott (1968) telling us that it is primarily affective rather than rational and its most frequently cited aspect is an individual's sense of what is right or wrong, appropriate or inappropriate in a given context. Following this thought takes us to Norman's account of the kinds of emotional responses we have to digital technology. Norman (2004) claims that these visceral or intuitive responses are both unlearned and are independent of culture.

3.7.2   INTUITION AND PERCEPTION

Kant (1748) was perhaps the first to describe intuition as having perception-like qualities and Davidson (1882, p. 304) has offered a complementary etymological perspective writing that "Intuition literally means—seeing though the eye, visual perception […] If, then, we ask at this stage what

Intuition is, we obtain as answer—the apprehension or discerning of a thing actually present to the eye; and it is distinguished, on the one hand, from the revival of that thing in memory ...." Thus Davidson defines intuitiveness as perception in action. Dreyfus would agree as he does not distinguish between perception and action.

It was, of course, Gibson (1977, 1986) who elucidated this action-perception coupling. For Gibson, perception is not mediated by internal representations instead it has evolved to detect and exploit the opportunities which the environment provides. "We must perceive in order to move, but we must also move in order to perceive" (1979, p. 223). This position has received both support and attention with work in the cognitive sciences (e.g., Clark, 1997a), robotics (e.g., Schaal, 1999), the study of skilled behaviour (e.g., Montagne et al., 2003) and developmental psychology (e.g., Thelen and Smith, 1994; Bertenthal et al., 1997). Together this work has underlined the unmediated coupling between perception and action. However, for the sake of the current argument, we wish to highlight a less familiar aspect of perception, namely that it is the product of experience. Wartofsky (1979) has long treated perception as an historical process having been culturally acquired and one that continues to expand with additional individual or group experience. Before we consider his argument, the idea that perception might have a history is easily grasped by way of example: consider an X-ray image. Traditionally these comprise patterns of light and dark which fall, correspondingly, onto our retinas as patterns of light and dark. To the untrained eye these are relatively meaningless, but to the practiced clinician they may signal the health of the heart and lungs.

Wartofsky's argument begins, like Gibson's treatment of affordance, with the recognition that perception is a functional aspect of the interactions between animals and their environments. He observes that there is a reciprocal relationship between the animal and its environment: while the perceived world of the animal can be treated as a map or an image of the animal's activities, the senses of animals themselves are shaped by the purposive interactions which the species has with the environment, or as he puts it, "Rather, the very forms of perceptual activity are now shaped to, and also help to shape an environment created by conscious human activity itself. This environment is the world made by praxis."

Examples of this kind of perception in action in these artefactual worlds include the chess board, the disposition of which an expert can understand with a glance (e.g., Chase and Simon, 1973). Research indicates that historic perception may also be at work when navigating an academic paper (e.g., Dillon and Scaap, 1996) and predicting the direction of an opponent's tennis serve (e.g., Farrow and Abernethy, 2003). A further excellent example of this may be found in Goodwin and Goodwin's (1998) study of operational staff at an airport. The study demonstrates how perceptions of information artefacts (flight information displays, documentation linking flights, destinations and aircraft) and their perceived properties or characteristics are shaped by the histories of both the personnel involved and the artefacts themselves. The Goodwins further observe that such perceptions are always grounded in particular organisations, tasks, and mediating artefacts.

3.8   AN INITIAL SKETCH OF COPING

Jeff Raskin (1994) directly equates familiarity with intuitiveness. In a brief essay on what intuitive means, he wrote that a user interface is "intuitive" in as much as it resembles (or is identical) to something the user already knows, "In short, intuitive in this context is an almost exact synonym of familiar." In contrast, Simonton (1980, p. 6) defines intuition as, "behavioural adaptations to the environment which tend to be unconscious, ineffable, and essentially probabilistic in character" and Noddings and Shore (1984) tell us that intuitive behaviour is characteristic in familiar domains. They also observe that the greater the familiarity the more likely and reliable the intuitions. Dreyfus et al. (1988), writing that, "intuition is the product of deep situational involvement and recognition of similarity" (p. 28). Blackler and her colleagues (e.g., Blackler and Hurtienne, 2007) argues that intuition is an unconscious form of cognition reliant on prior practical knowledge, and Reason and Mycielska (1982, p. 224) go further by suggesting that familiar objects in themselves will actually trigger automatic behaviour, "... familiar objects possess what we call an immediate controlling region. Once in touch with them, our actions conform to the structural needs of the object."

In summary, intuition is the result from the repeated exposure to familiar situations, and intuitive behaviour is triggered by these self-same familiar situations. In recognising this we can bring together and distinguish between familiarity and intuitiveness. These are not identical as Raskin would have us believe but familiarity is our preparedness to cope and intuition is that preparedness in execution: together this is coping. Familiarity and intuitiveness are not synonyms but are the two faces of the same underlying cognitive process. Figure 3.2 is a preliminary sketch of coping based on what we have considered so far. Being-in-the-world results in our familiarity with it, which readies us to cope with digital technology. This familiarity (prior knowledge and "know-how") is put to use intuitively, that is, quickly, automatically and without deliberation.

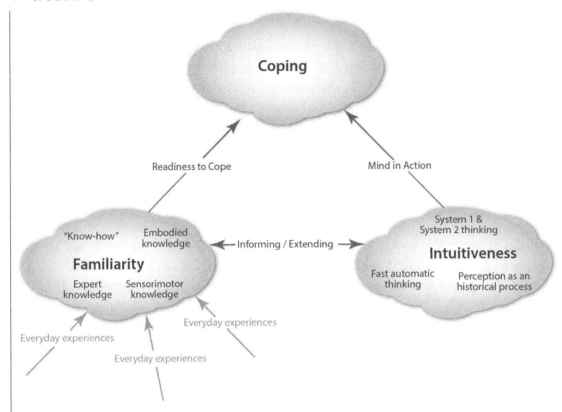

Figure 3.2: A preliminary sketch of coping.

3.9   IN SUMMARY

Coping is practical intelligence; coping is mind in action; coping is that form of everyday thinking which deals effectively with a messy world which, as Rogoff (1984) notes, " […] is not illogical or sloppy but instead is sensible and effective in handling practical problems." Scribner (1986) also describes this kind of practical thinking as "mind in action" by which she means, "thinking that is embedded in the larger purposive activities of daily life and that function to achieve the goals of those activities" (p. 15). This kind of thinking she further describes as instrumental, that is, specifically directed at achieving goals and as being completely distinct from the type of thinking involved in the performance of isolated mental tasks undertaken as ends in themselves.

Is Coping Automatic?

We all recognise that we perform routine activities quickly with little or no thought or awareness—automatically. So, is coping automatic? In brief, it is not but it does have elements which may be automatic. Schenider and his colleagues have observed that our every-day behaviour is the result of two processes which they describe as being either automatic or controlled (**Schneider and Shiffrin, 1977**; and **Shiffrin and Schneider, 1977**; **Schneider et al., 1984**). This is not to be understood as a mutually exclusive either-or but an intermix, with people alternating between automatic and controlled processing. These researchers also distinguished between these processes in terms of the demands they made on our attention. Automatic processing is being fast, difficult to modify (as it is not under direct control), but makes no demands on our attentional resources. As such, automatic processing is confined to well-developed, familiar tasks. In contrast, controlled processing is slow, under conscious control, effortful, and capacity-limited. We rely on controlled processing in unfamiliar sit-uations. Shiffrin and his colleagues regarding automaticity as being the result of repeated or habitual exposure and of controlled processes. Ericsson and Simon (**1984**) agree, telling us that attention is not required when the same cognitive process has been executed many times.

Other accounts of automatic and controlled behaviour exist, each solving a particular prob-lem. In the context of the skilled use of technology, Rasmussen's (**1983**) Skill, Rule, and Knowledge model distinguishes between what he describes as sensory-motor performance, which "takes place without conscious control as smooth, automated, and highly integrated patterns of behavior" from those which are rule-based or knowledge-based. Another related account of automatic behaviour can be found in Norman's Activation-Trigger-Schema (ATS) proposal (**Norman, 1981**). In this he offers an explanation as to how people can encounter a familiar situation, recognise it, and act without deliberation. For example, when driving, the appropriate sequences of actions for braking or steering are triggered automatically (at least in the experienced driver) by appropriate conditions such as traffic lights, oncoming traffic, and so forth. Norman's ATS model proposes that action sequences such as these are realised by sensorimotor schemata, which are trigger by activated higher level schema. Once triggered these lower-level components complete the action autono-mously, without the further need for intervention. The parallel with hierarchical structure of an activity, as defined by Activity Theory, is striking (**Operations**). Overall, while coping may share some of the characteristics of automatic behaviour, the fact that it is intrinsically adaptive means that it cannot be reduced to mere automaticity.

Operations

Activity Theory is a body of thought which has been developed from the work of Marx, and Ilyenkov and the cultural-historical psychology of Vygostki, Leontev, and Luria. It has also been proposed as a theory for human-computer interaction, computer supported cooperative work, and user-centred design (e.g., **Bødker, 1991**; **Kuutti, 1996**; **Nardi, 1996** among others).

Kaptelinin (**1997**) describes Activity Theory as having five defining characteristics, which are: (a) object-orientation; (b) mechanisms for internalisation-externalisation; (c) a hierarchical structure (activity-action-operation); (d) the role of (tool) mediation; and (e) development (learning).

Our interest here is in the hierarchical structure. At the highest level of the hierarchy are activities. Activities have a motive (or *object*, hence the *object*-orientation) that is realised by means of a group of actions which have their own individual goals. Actions, in turn, are realised by means of operations. Operations are automatic, internalised, and triggered by suitable conditions (**Kuutti, 1996** p. 38). In short, operations are situated.

Further, while they are not consciously performed they originally were under conscious control (cf. internalisation-externalisation). Bærentsen and Trettvik (**2002**) tell us that "They [operations] result from appropriated use of tools, educated manners toward other human beings, or movements in the physical world according to concrete physical conditions." Operations begin as sequences of behaviour that are under conscious control (that is, they begin as actions) but with increasing familiarity and practice, actions cease to be under conscious control and are demoted or "pushed down" the hierarchy to become an operation. This is illustrated in **Figure 2.2**.

Figure 3.3: The hierarchical structure of an activity.

Operations are performed unconsciously. This is not to suggest that operations are frozen; they remain responsive to the conditions of the environment, indeed, operations are "triggered" by the demands of the situation. From this description it does seem likely that operations play an important role in coping.

CHAPTER 4

Epistemic Scaffolding

4.1 KEY POINTS

- Coping is our flexible, adaptive response to the demands of the world. Coping is how we deal with digital technology.

- Coping is frequently scaffolded by epistemic actions. The term "epistemic action" is borrowed from cognitive science and refers to actions that make completing a task easier, faster, or more reliable.

- Epistemic actions are not about achieving our goals directly but instead act as prompts, aids, supports, and to use our preferred word, *scaffolding*. A very simple example is the use of a shopping list. Creating a shopping list does not directly aid the process of shopping but does help us remember what to buy.

- Epistemic actions involve making intelligent use of the environment (e.g., using the apparent chaos on an untidy desk to date documents—the oldest being at the bottom of the heap), the use of language both private (as self-talk) and public (used to redefine and simplify problems), external representations (the use of charts, diagrams, and signage) and help from other people (e.g., "how do you switch this on?" and teaching children to tie their shoelaces).

- Epistemic actions may also involve personalising, configuring, and appropriating the technology itself to reflect how we wish to use it. These acts of appropriation can range from the slight (e.g., the use of wallpaper) through to actively modifying or even re-designing the technology itself as our understanding and changing needs ("design-in-use").

- We propose the concept of a technological niche to complement the existing work in artefact ecologies. It is argued that we actively create niches that insulate us from the unwanted pressure and complexities of technology. These niches may be ephemeral and contingent or well established and institutional. These niches work because they are familiar.

4.2   WHEN COPING ALONE IS NOT ENOUGH

So far we have argued that we cope because we have acquired the necessary "know-how" and familiarity to deal with what we encounter—whether it be digital or otherwise. Moreover we have established that we cope without recourse to deliberation. (Dreyfus and Valera being very definitely of this opinion, while Wheeler's position is more equivocal). Yet, we are not automata simply responding to the stimuli offered by the everyday world or thoughtlessly accepting every invitation offered by an affordance as it is clear that our behaviour is very frequently supported, nudged, and helped along by other factors. The first half of this chapter discusses these "other factors" for which we adopt the term "epistemic actions."

We begin by defining these actions and then consider a number of different examples of them which feature as part of our everyday coping. These examples are drawn from both the HCI and cognitive science literature and have been chosen to reflect their ubiquity in everyday life.

In the second half of this chapter (Section 4.7 and onwards) we continue this theme but highlight an important difference between epistemic actions in general and those which are more peculiar to digital technology: of these are the various acts of appropriation by which we make the technology our own. We appropriate digital technology in a variety of different ways a *subset of which* is to make it easier to use—which, as we shall see, is the definition of an epistemic action.

Adding a role for the epistemic to the notion of coping results in a kind of hybrid vigour for the account as a whole while, of course, running the risk of being seen as a (potential) contradiction in terms. The case for epistemic scaffolding is made at length in this chapter but in brief:

1. There is abundant empirical evidence to support such a position, for example, shopping for groceries is scaffolded by means of a shopping list; personalising my computer desktop makes it easier to find the applications I wish to use; and using a playlist on an MP3 player allows us to skip the tracks we don't like. Scaife and Rogers (1996) have described how these kinds of actions as "computational off-loading." While Sutton and his colleagues (2011) have also written convincingly of "instructional nudges" and "self-talk" serving the same purpose in the skilled performances of sports people;

2. As these epistemic actions are available (that is, they do not require deliberation to use) they act as part of the wider cognitive system. This is consistent with the "extended self" hypothesis which has considerable traction within cognitive science and, as we shall see, is consistent with formulations of distributed and situated cognition within HCI;

3. Coping comprises our repertoire of adaptive skills and this means being responsive to the situation and making best use of those resources which are ready-to-hand to reach our goals; finally,

4. The appropriation of technology is most usually associated with an ever growing list of such issues as preferences, personalisation, re-use, sustainability, self-presentation … and to this list we focus on changing the technology to better suit what we want to do with it. This aspect of appropriation is reflexive and epistemic: we actively change the technology itself to make it easier to achieve our goals.

4.3   DEFINING EPISTEMIC ACTIONS

Epistemic actions were first defined by Kirsh and Maglio (1994) as a result of their analysis of how people play Tetris. Tetris is a tile-matching video game. The game requires the player to rotate falling tiles before dropping them into the matrix of tiles below. On filling a row, it disappears affording the player more time and space to continue playing the game. Kirsh and Maglio were primarily interested in how people solve these cognitive and perceptual problems in real time as the tiles fall. Their assumption was that the tiles were subject to mental rotation by the player before they used the controls to position the tile. This mental rotation is quite a demanding task, particularly as it is time pressured. What they actually found was the some of the translations and rotations made by players employed the actual playing environment itself to ease the load on the player's cognition. Most importantly, these actions in themselves were not part of a plan (to continue playing the game and achieving a high score) but served to simplify the problem-solving task itself. On this basis these researchers were able to distinguish between what they describe as pragmatic actions, which are performed to bring the player closer to achieving their goal or goals, from epistemic actions, which are performed to "uncover information that is hidden or hard to compute mentally." They also define epistemic actions as "physical actions that make mental computation easier, faster or more reliable—are external actions that an agent performs to change its own computational state" (1994, p. 4) and, "[they are] actions designed to change the input to an agent's information processing system. They are ways an agent had of modifying the external environment to provide crucial bits of information just when they need it most" (1994, p. 38). Clark (2008, p. 73) describes the relationship between pragmatic and epistemic actions as one of, "active dovetailing."

Related studies have revealed similar use of the environment to simplify problem solving in people playing Scrabble™ and children playing with Montessori blocks. In both cases the tiles/blocks were arranged and re-arranged to *help* with the task rather than as a means to complete the task directly (Klemmer et al., 2006). In short, epistemic actions serve to reduce cognitive load, to make completing a task simpler and quicker and, as we shall see, can be found everywhere.

4.4   ABDUCTION

Given the ubiquity of epistemic actions it is reasonable to consider their origins. A simple answer is that we invent them (by means of *abduction*).

The philosopher C. S. Peirce proposed *abduction* as a new, third form of reasoning (in addition to deduction and induction). Unlike these other forms, abduction is the process of inferring facts, laws, regularities, patterns, and hypotheses that explain or disclose some (eventually new) phenomenon or observation; it is the process of reasoning in which explanatory hypotheses are formed and evaluated (Pierce, 5.171). So, scientific discovery can be seen as a process that relies on abduction. Abduction, in the current context, also describes those inferences that disclose new affordances in a technological artefact and, in doing so, afford the appropriation of that artefact. Rowe (1991, p. 38) noting that, "abduction is not a random process. The appropriation that is made must show promise in facilitating problem solving activity." Abduction is the only logical operation that actually introduces new ideas.

Magnani and Bardone (2008) have extended this concept to distinguish between theoretical and manipulative abduction. The former is described as creative reasoning (as found in scientific reasoning) while manipulative abduction they characterise as "discovering through doing" or "thinking through doing." They argue that manipulation (doing) can provide access to otherwise unavailable information, which then enables the individual to generate or select abductive hypotheses. Manipulative abduction occurs when external artefacts are transformed into "cognitive mediators" that give rise to new opportunities and new interpretations. They also (ibid, pp. 10-12) note that manipulative abductive reasoning can create epistemic templates, for example: manipulation can simplify a task when we are in the "presence of redundant and unmanageable information"; it can also provide forms of information (e.g., tactile and visual) otherwise unavailable (Thinking with Our Hands).

4.5   EPISTEMIC ACTIONS AT WORK

This section offers a necessarily incomplete though broad sampling of the different kinds of *epistemic action*. The intention is not to create a definite list of its many tropes but to illustrate their ubiquity. We consider examples from computer-supported cooperative working (CSCW) through to the "intelligent use of space," help from other people, and the role of language. We should note that these different kinds of epistemic actions fall into (or can be arranged into) different categories all of which overlap in largely unhelpful ways.

Further, there is a substantial literature on how organisations appropriate technology to suit the ways in which they choose to work, and indeed the first example we consider is typical of this. However we will not dwell on these because of their strongly organisational and information systems character which is not particularly relevant to our argument.

4.5.1   EPISTEMIC ACTIONS AS ARTICULATION

The discipline of CSCW considers the social organisation of work and how information technology might support it. After decades of research it emerges that CSCW fundamentally relies on the three mechanisms of coordination, mutual awareness, and articulation. While coordination and awareness are not unexpected components, articulation needs a little explanation.

Schmidt and Bannon (1992) were arguably the first researchers to recognise that cooperative work implies an overhead "in terms of labor, resources, time" compared with individual work. They recognised that cooperative work involves a number of supporting activities that mediated these individual, cooperative parts. For example, tasks have to be allocated to individual workers and they have to be instructed as to what to do, where, when, and with whom. In short, these cooperating workers have to be articulated with respect to their distributed individual activities.

Bowers (1994) described articulation work (in the context of getting a computer network to function) as "the work to make the network work," which he said is not to be dismissed as infrastructural or as merely "oiling the wheels." Indeed Bowers had identified a class of endeavour that was required to ensure that the main focus of work was both achievable and achieved. Subsequent research found widespread examples of this kind of *articulation work* the characteristics of which has been most fully described by Schmidt and Simone (1996). They begin by describing cooperative work as the interplay between multiple people working individually but through their interaction changing the state of a common body of work. However as this work is inherently distributed, other kinds of work must be undertaken to ensure that this cooperative work, works. They write, "To deal with this […] individual and yet interdependent activities must be coordinated, scheduled, aligned, meshed, integrated, etc.—in short, articulated. They primarily see articulation work (lit. "put together by joints") as the means by which the orderly accomplishment of cooperative work is achieved. And, of course, this may have a recursive aspect to it as articulation work is itself cooperative. Articulation work can then be seen as comprising those epistemic actions which ensure that the focus of the cooperative work is made easier (i.e., "scheduled, aligned, meshed, and so forth").

Perhaps the most striking examples of articulation work can be found in studies involving the real-time coordination and awareness required of air traffic controllers. Bentley et al. (1992), among many others, have reported on the use of flight strips to articulate the work of this group. A flight strip is a strip of paper annotated with key details of a particular aircraft (including destination, heading, speed and so forth). Flight strips are organised on a flight progress board where they are aligned and organised according to the reporting points over which a flight will pass. These strips allow the experienced controller to become aware "at a glance" of the disposition of the airspace. While flight strips are not directly involved controlling or directing aircraft, they do make it less cognitively demanding.

4.5.2   USING THE ENVIRONMENT

Malone (1983) who (optimistically) sought to find an automated means to a tidy desk, has reported a study of how people organise their office desks. He found that the state of the desk itself provided reminders of the things that the owner of the desk had to do. For example, Malone's interview with the (messy) research scientist "Kenneth" revealed that "Beside my terminal […] are basically piles of stuff about what I need in hacking in the recent past. The deeper you go, the further back it is. Off to the right is stuff that I've shoved to the right when the pile beside my terminal got too high. But I've periodically pruned it so it's no longer useful; it's just a pile of junk …" (p. 103). Malone takes pains to emphasise that "Kenneth" is not disorganised but that he uses the spatial organisation of the different piles of paperwork to remind him of where (and when) he was with different aspects of his work. In subsequent research, Wells (2000) has also underlined the importance of being able to personalise one's workspace for an individual's sense of well-being and job-satisfaction.

In a different sphere Clark (2001) has reported on how skilled cocktail waiters take pains to organise the layout of the bottles of spirits and other ingredients they require to make a cocktail to match the temporal sequence of their use (e.g., begin by adding crushed ice, then add a measure of rum followed by …). The spatial ordering of the bottles and other ingredients helps the waiter to remember the sequence of the recipe.

In what has become something of a seminal paper, Kirsh (1995a) has described examples such as these as the intelligent use of space. The data for this study were variously drawn from a number of diverse sources including "videos of cooking, assembly and packing, everyday observations in supermarkets, workshops and playrooms" (p. 34). One example of this is the description of someone preparing an elaborate salad. The cook in question began by cutting each of the fruits and vegetables into thin slices and placing them in neat piles. These were then arranged on large platter along the circumference. When asked, the cook said that their aim was to dress the platter with the fruits and vegetables in a "uniform and aesthetic manner" and without running out of any one ingredient until they were all used up.

Table 4.1 is taken from this reported work and offers a flavour of his findings. In this instance Kirsh has identified a number of different strategies (epistemic actions), which people adopt to simplify and reduce the burden on specific aspects of our cognition.

Table 4.1: After Kirsh 1995a, p. 66		
Capacity improved	**What has been reduced**	**Mechanism**
Recall	Probability of an error in prospective memory	Reminders
Visual search	Time complexity of search Descriptive complexity of environment Probability of an error	Use known ordering such as chucks or alphabets
Reasoning	Time complexity of planning	Cue next action though a known ordering
Execution	Probability of capture error	Maximise cue separation

Perhaps the most novel example of this intelligent use of space concerns the ways in which set (stage) design in Elizabethan plays scaffolds the actors' memories of the plot itself. Tribble (2011) tells us that a repertory company of players of that time would typically be expected to perform six plays every week with very few repeat performances. She has observed that the availability of the doors—opening onto and affording egress from the stage—helped the actors to remember what to do next (enter stage left, speak lines, exit stage second door to the right—all other doors being locked). Thus the stage and its players, props and so forth comprise what she and Sutton describe as a "cognitive ecology" in which "we remember, feel, think, sense, communicate, imagine, and act, often collaboratively, on the fly, and in rich on going interaction with our environments" (Tribble and Sutton, 2011).

4.5.3   MAKING USE OF EXTERNAL REPRESENTATIONS

Figure 4.1 is an image of a familiar scene, a note secured to a monitor to remind an office worker to carry out specific tasks everyday and one particular task on a Friday. Creating and using these notes does not directly contribute to completing the task of "emailing MLs to remind them about feedback" but again they do make it easier to remember.

The use of external representation range from the mundane use of shopping lists (supporting our limited and error-prone memory) through to the scientist's use of a specialised notation (capturing complex ideas in a few pen strokes) to model the completeness of, say, a safety critical design. Neither the shopping list in itself, nor the use of a specialised notation, guarantee the successful completion of these task but as Kirsh (1995a, p. 34) puts it, "people make mental tools of things in the environment", while Lave (1977) uses the term "environmental calculating devices" to capture the same idea. These examples of abduction are evidence that people find it easier to solve the problems situated in the real world by drawing upon available resources, rather than relying on cognitively demanding computation.

Figure 4.1: Office reminders.

At this point we move our attention from the use of, and modifications to, the external environment to those epistemic actions which rely on language and other people.

4.6 PRIVATE AND PUBLIC LANGUAGE

First, a note: We recognise that Wittgenstein's linguistic philosophy makes use of the term "private language" in a very specific way and our usage here is different. By "private language" we mean that (i) it is not directed at an interlocutor and that (ii) it is the internalised form of the external "public" variety.

For Clark, the most important epistemic artefact is language, describing it as "a tool that alters the nature of the computational tasks involved in various kinds of problem solving" and, "in many ways the ultimate artefact" (Clark, 1997b, p. 193 & p. 218 respectively). We use language to redefine problems thus simplifying our coping with the world (p. 168). He goes on to identify six different ways in which language redefines problems so as to scaffold our coping. His first two examples are particularly familiar: language lends itself to memory augmentation by way of texts, diaries, and notebooks. Language also helps with environmental simplification, examples of which include signage and the components of a graphical user interface (e.g., menus, icons). He continues in much the same vein citing the usefulness of language to aid coordination, help with managing the demands on our attention and so forth.

4.6.1   SELF-TALK & INSTRUCTIONAL NUDGES

Imagine entering a column of numbers into a spreadsheet, after entering the tenth entry we have to insert a blank row and then continue. Many of us in performing this task would count aloud. Or we have five items to buy from a supermarket, again I for one would vocalise (or sub vocalise) this list, bananas, bread, beer, bacon and beetroot .... bananas, bread, beer, bacon, and beetroot. We are scaffolding these simple, routine tasks by talking to ourselves. Sutton et al. (2011) calls this "self-talk" and recognises similar behaviour has been observed in a number of different contexts ranging from sports to jazz music. Sudnow (2001), in his *Ways of the Hand: A Rewritten Account*, offers an auto-ethnography of learning to play jazz piano. In this he writes of self-talk as "nudges." He writes (p. 128), "I can institute jazz handling by telling myself—looking at my hand and composing its appearance over the course of play for a pose to satisfy the look which asks—'let me see jazz hands!' Telling myself 'let me see jazz hands' works as a nudge."

Sutton et al. (2011) offers a further example of this self-talk based on a series of interviews with cricketers. Sutton and his colleagues found that these sportsmen talked to themselves before playing a shot. Cricketers report that they tell themselves to "watch the ball" and to "play straight", before every ball bowled to them. Sutton tells us that this should not be regarded as a preparatory tactic between periods of deliberation, as the cricketer himself tells us, "I usually say that just as the bowler's heading up into his delivery stride. So that's at the point of delivery" (quoted by Sutton et al., 2011, p. 92).

Sutton describes the function of these verbal nudges as "a material symbol, an iterated and interactive self-stimulatory loop." We should bear in mind that a cricket ball is typically bowled at 120-150 kilometres per hour and the batman has typically less than 0.4s to respond. Acting within 0.4s is typical of immediate coping but does not allow for reflection. Wheeler (2005) agrees and suggests that the role of "instructional nudges" cannot be about the precise control of the action taken, instead the skilled individual is using these nudges "to distribute intelligence, coordinating or often re-setting and re-chunking patterns of movement or affect or mood, as one among many forms of scaffolding." Thus these "other factors" are not the sources of our practical coping with technology but help link the appropriate form of that coping and with its execution.

Heath and Luff (1992; 2000) have reported several examples of this public/private use of language in their studies of complex real time working environments. They found that staff in situations as diverse as a London underground control room and a Reuters newsroom, were found to monitor "out louds" and other verbal asides as part of their work. In the case of the London underground, the overall controller made his work (including his reasoning and individual behaviour) visible by talking "out loud." This talk is not directed at a particular colleague within the control room—which might entail a subsequent conversation, and would necessarily divert attention away from individual tasks—instead this is a form of "self-talk" directed at, perhaps, the train timetable. This monitoring alerted staff to changes to the system without interrupting their own work.

4.6.2   THE ZONE OF PROXIMAL DEVELOPMENT

Although there are potentially many ways of discussing the role of language in coping, it was Vygotski (1978; 1986) who best articulated the relationship between private and public language in his treatment of the Zone of Proximal Development (ZPD). The ZPD is defined as "The distance between the actual development level as determined by independent problem solving and the level of potential development as determined through problem solving under adult guidance or in collaboration with more capable peers." Consider a child trying to tie her shoelaces. We can imagine the struggle she might have if this challenge were beyond her abilities. Naturally she turns to a parent or teacher to help. We might expect the adult to demonstrate the process, or guide the child through the process with a running dialogue (or perhaps even accompanied by a rhyme involving *bunny ears*). Later when the child needs to retie a loose lace she can repeat what she was instructed but this time to herself. The public language of the adult, having been successfully internalised, now functions to guide behaviour. Vygotski has argued, using examples such as this, that the use of public language has profound effects on cognitive development. Vygotski tells us, "Every function in the child's cultural development appears twice: first, on the social level, and later, on the individual level; first, between people (inter-psychological) and then inside the child (intra-psychological). This applies equally to voluntary attention, to logical memory, and to the formation of concepts. All the higher functions originate as actual relationships between individuals."

The ZPD is not merely a product of child-adult relationships as it is always with us. Every time we ask for help from a more skilled, knowledgeable, or the nearest available person, we can see these mechanisms at work. Indeed when coping is not quite enough we do not simply experience an all or nothing breakdown (cf. Wheeler's discussion of *unavailability* in Chapter 3), instead we rely on epistemic nudges to allow us to continue to engage with the technology.

This can be seen in the following example. I witnessed a pair of young backpackers at the central railway station in Amsterdam trying to use a left luggage locker (they were immediately ahead of me in the queue, I had both a good view of them and could hear what they were saying and I have a long history of surreptitiously watching people struggling with technology). They selected the picture of the British flag on the system's user interface and the display was promptly rendered into English. The instructions told them to do the following: choose a locker of the appropriate size, put the luggage inside, close the door, insert money (or credit card & PIN), and then wait for a receipt. The receipt providing the number they would need to unlock the locker and retrieve their luggage. This sequence is a familiar one and from a usability perspective the sequence was clearly logical and well documented. However from the perspective of these backpackers, the situation appeared to be fraught and uncertain. As I waited my turn, I tried to imagine the source of their dithering and I could not help but wonder if the backpackers think that the operators of the left luggage lockers are going to steal their credit card details? Could the system be trusted? However within a few seconds the situation was resolved by the pair asking a nearby successful user of the system whether it was "ok." He replied, "Yeah, it's ok." Not help as such, more of a nudge.

4.7   THE APPROPRIATION OF DIGITAL TECHNOLOGY

In this lecture we have argued that we cope with digital technology in much the same way as we use all other kinds of everyday technology and in the first half of this chapter we identified a role for epistemic actions in scaffolding this coping. These examples have shown that scaffolding can take a variety of forms but we now intend taking one step further by proposing that some aspects of the appropriation of digital technology may have an epistemic aspect too.

Our argument begins by recognising that digital technology differs in one important respect from other everyday technology, namely, we appropriate it. By appropriation we mean that we make it our own by changing it, personalising it, configuring it, and so forth. This is not to say that we do not personalise other forms of everyday technology but that it is a matter of ubiquity (everyone does it) and that digital technology specifically lends itself to appropriation. Digital technology has a malleability, pliability, configurability, compliance, and flexibility (there probably isn't a single word which captures all of this) which invites people to make it their own and this is simply not true, to anything like the same extent, of other forms of everyday technology. It is difficult to imagine anyone who uses their mobile phone, laptop, or tablet computer as is, that is, unchanged from the moment they bought it, while the converse is largely true of other kinds of everyday technology. Even if our working environment prescribes a particular technology with its standard software image, we appropriate our broader working environment to ameliorate these constraints (cf. Malone, 1983). But this too is changing with an increasing number of employers encouraging "bring your own technology" to the workplace (BBC, 2012).

While we agree that appropriation is more usually seen as a matter of self-expression and preference, it should also be recognised that we appropriate digital technology in order to meet our needs. Needs which can take a variety of forms: functional, aesthetic, social, ludic, or as an expression of who we are. From this perspective, acts of appropriation may have an epistemic dimension.

More than this, to appropriate digital technology is to engage in a *reflexive epistemic* action in which the technology itself is reshaped.

This is an extension of Kirsh and Maglio's original vision but, as we shall see, it is one which is consistent with their work.

4.7.1   WHAT IS DEEMED NOT TO BE APPROPRIATION

Before we embark on our discussion of appropriation, we need to say a few words on what we do not regard as examples of appropriation. Broadly we do not include the results of user modelling or customisation to be appropriation. The key difference between these endeavours and appropriation lies with the reflexive nature of making technology our own. We define appropriation as something we do to technology whereas when other people (designers or just the well meaning) change technology to better suit us, it is the consequence of user modelling (formally or informally) and results in customisation rather than appropriation. This distinction is best seen by way of an example. In England, training wheels are called stabilisers and refer to a extra set of small wheels attached to the rear wheel of a bicycle to add stability for the learner rider. The concept was introduce to the HCI community by Carroll and Carrithers (1984) who designed a training wheels interface for a commercial word processor.

In brief, they firstly catalogued the range of errors new users made. They then modified the system's interface to block these errors; for example, the authors identified the "Exotic Menu Choice Error" that involved novice users "recklessly try[ing] out menu choices in their early encounters with the system." This error was removed by making this menu choice unavailable. The training wheels interface offered a simplification (by a third party) of the available choices to the new user.

While we do not take issue with the usefulness of this approach, the authors did undertake an analysis of novice user behaviour and modified the technology in the light of that and for these reasons we do not regard this to be an example of appropriation.

Further examples of customisation include modifying technology to meet the requirements, needs, desires and wishes of the elderly or disabled (e.g., Worden et al., 1997; Gregor et al., 2002; among many others). Again there is a model, underlying this behaviour, of how these groups might best be served by technology which is correspondingly customised to meet these expectations.

4.8   THE DIMENSIONS OF APPROPRIATION

We take appropriation to be an umbrella term encompassing user configuration, "do-it-yourself" design, ensoulment, and personalisation. None of these categories have widely agreed definitions and as such tend to overlap but this is less important than recognising, just like *epistemic actions*, the sheer variety of forms appropriation can take.

4.8.1   USER CONFIGURATION

In the context of digital technology, Maclean and his colleagues tell us that the first user-tailorable systems were the Xerox graphical user interfaces which allowed their users to reposition on-screen buttons to suit themselves (MacLean et al., 1990). We now, of course, routinely modify the toolbars available with office applications; we populate our smartphones with "apps" and we re-configure the controls within games. Beyond these fairly simple acts, appropriation itself has become a matter of academic interest. It is usual to quote Dourish at this point. Dourish (2003) defines appropriation as "the way in which technologies are adopted, adapted and incorporated into working practice" but prior to this, Silverstone and Haddon (1996) coined the term "domestication" to describe the ways in which technologies are integrated into everyday life and adapted to match the demands of daily practices. They based these ideas on the domestication of wild animals for their use as sources of food, clothing, work, and protection. Domestication not only changes the lives of these animals but the ways in which we deal with our everyday lives (e.g., riding rather than walking). Silverman describes the stages of the domestication of technology as beginning with it being integrated into everyday life and adapted to daily practices, this is followed by the users adapting accordingly, which may, in turn, be followed by the adoption of these adaptations and innovations by the manufacturers of the technology. The cycle then repeats.

More recently Belin and Prié (2012) extended this discussion to recognise it as the process by which people continuously integrate artefacts into their practices, which they see as completing the work of the designer. This is appropriation as design-in-use (e.g., Dix, 2007; Salovaara, 2008). They recognise that appropriation occurs in response to the situated demands users encounter. From this perspective, appropriation reflects the evolution of the digital artefact itself.

Continuing this theme of appropriation as design-in-use, recent years have witnessed a growing interest in what has been described as do-it-yourself (DIY) design. This has taken a variety of forms including: design for serendipity (Newman et al., 2002); design for sustainability (e.g., Blevis, 2007); designing for hackability (Galloway et al., 2004) together with the ad hoc creation of "mash-ups" (Zang et al., 2008).

4.8.2   ENSOULMENT

Ensoulment is a distinctive form of appropriation. Nelson and Stolterman (2003) define it to mean, "promot[ing] an aesthetic of well-loved designs in which the meaning and value of a design is taken in as a feeling of being deeply moved and as a consequence, a feeling of being significantly changed." Ensouled things are things that are and have been cared for, looked after, and valued. For ensoulment to occur the everyday designer must be open to interpretation as to the purpose, function, and re-interaction of the digital artefact. This aspect of appropriation is about designing (re-designing) artefacts that are adaptable to the user, empowering and reflecting the user's personal identity. Nelson and Stolterman thus redefine appropriation as the act of adapting an artefact to oneself in a way that not only redefines the artefact, but also relates the artefact to one's sense of self. (They define this sense of self or identity as the unique set of experiences, qualities, characteristics, thoughts, behaviours, and so forth which recognisably define an individual or collection of individuals, and the relationships occurring between them.)

Akah and Bardzell (2010) have also highlighted the relationship between personal identity and the appropriation of digital objects through the processes of bricolage (another variant on DIY design) and using examples from the Steampunk movement. Steampunk is a genre of 'modern' science fiction set in Victorian times. Examples include, Alan Moore's *The League of Extraordinary Gentlemen* (Moore and O'Neill, 2001) and Stephen Baxter's *Anti Ice*. Steampunk has also been described as a revival of the 19th Century Arts and Crafts Movement with its emphasis on hand-crafting. The politics (or aesthetics) of Steampunk are a rejection of the "always-connected", homogenized-commodities in favour of creating things of value and meaning by drawing inspiration from the Steam/Victorian age. So, the "steam punks" appropriate digital technology, in part, because it was not designed for them individually (Commodities and Things).

Commodities and Things

The American philosopher of technology Albert Borgmann (**1984**) has distinguished between commodities and things. He defines a commodity is a context-free entity isolated from traditions and customs. A thing, in contrast, is capable of engaging and connecting with us. So, for example, a pizza bought from a chain is an example of a commodity, whereas a home-cooked dinner is a thing. Pizza are uniform (e.g., 12 inches in diameter), safe, reliable, and quantifiable (though may be seen to be contributing to the homogenization of society); while a home-cooked dinner relies on the skill of the cook, the availability of ingredients, time, effort and is an experience not easily susceptible to quantification. One is packaged and delivered (in an cardboard box by a youth on a motorcycle) while the other is open to inspection, modification, and even participation.

As for digital artefacts we now buy and use mobile phones, laptops, MP3 players and so forth (often from supermarkets together with the weekly groceries) which are known to be safe, reliable, and usable without our necessarily having the remotest of ideas of how they work. Yet only a generation ago it was not only commonplace to tinker with one's personal computer but often an absolute necessity. Many of us will remember manually editing the start up and configuration files to resolve conflicts in, for example, loading devices into memory. Information technology, then, was a thing requiring familiarity with its operation. In contrast, today there is an increasing dichotomy between the user interface and the "black box" which lies beneath.

4.8.3 PERSONALISATION

Personalisation is the process by which an artefact is endowed with greater significance by and for its user and can be usefully seen as being a subset of appropriation. Wells (2000) defines it as "the deliberate decoration or modification of the environment" and associates it with "well-being." While Blom (2002) defines it as "a process that changes the functionality, interface, information content, or distinctiveness of a system to increase its personal relevance to an individual," Kirsh (2010, p. 3) observes that "The urge to use artifacts to project a social identity […] By owning or using a particular kind of tool a person represents himself or herself to be a certain kind of person […] People often feel that a tool's brand reputation confers prestige on its owner."

Blom and Monk (2003) have shown that personalising the appearance of artefacts has cognitive, social, and emotional dimensions. They describe the cognitive aspects of personalisation as improving of ease of use, better recognition of the system, and improved aesthetics (though this might have reasonably have been treated as a category in its own right as the research was concerned with personalizing the appearance of artefacts). The social dimensions of personalisation are concerned with reflecting personal and group identity. Finally, the largest category are the emotional effects on the user. These affective consequences include feelings of familiarity, ownership, control, fun, attachment, release from boredom, and other positive attachments.

We can personalise the ring-tone of our phones; we can buy personalised phone numbers; we can change the appearance of our phones and have them set with precious stones. In addition to personalising the appearance and aesthetics of our everyday technologies we can also add functionality. Default games controllers can be replaced with more realistic (though plastic) sniper rifles for use in combat games; musical "games" can be played using a guitar-shaped controller to simulate the real thing. Other personalised controllers include skateboards, steering wheels, boxing gloves, and inevitably, a light sabre. While recognising that personalisation increases the sense of ownership of the artefact and allowing people to express the aspirational or the playful sides of their character, it undoubtedly has a significant epistemic core too—it makes digital technology both more fun and easier to use.

4.9   TECHNOLOGICAL NICHES?

As we have already discussed in this chapter, we constantly seek to reduce the load on our cognition by delegating and distributing it across the environment, but Magnani and Bardone (2008, p. 3) go further and argue that we specifically, "build models, representations and other mediating structures" and that we are "ecological engineers" engaged in creating "cognitive niches." So, is what we are doing akin to this when we scaffold our everyday coping with digital technology?

Laland and Sterelny (2006) write, "The defining characteristic of niche construction is not organism-driven modification of the environment per se, but rather modification of the relationship between an organism and its relative niche. Hence the term "niche construction" includes such things as habitat selection, where organisms relocate in space to modify the environment that they experience" (p. 1751). Niches are found throughout the biological world, for example, beavers construct dams; ants, birds and primates build nests; territories are carefully marked out by a variety of animals and migratory routes have been well established. Niches are also found in the cognitive and epistemic worlds and in each instance they are concerned with organisms managing, optimising, and defining their local environment. So, do we create, to coin a phrase, *technological niches*, which might extend beyond the technology itself, wherein we feel comfortable and are able to cope with the complexity of the technology? Perhaps these "places" reflect an individual's "comfort zone", to adopt a popular expression. From this perspective technological niches may indeed be physically instantiated but also may reflect the existential. A technological niche may also be thought of as being *where* someone feels able to appropriate technology for their own purposes and as such this might be a social setting, sitting quietly alone, or killing time on train journey. In many respects these appropriative acts are an active expression of familiarity—we are make technology more familiar.

A technological niche can be created on demand, reflecting our minute-by-minute embodied use of the space around us or might have a more institutional, established character as illustrated in Figure 4.2. As for the former, Dalton et al. (2012) offer a nice example of this kind of ad hoc behaviour in a study of their Kolab system. They describe Kolab as a "nomadic TUI [tangible user interface] that takes advantage of the fact that the world is full of potential tangibles and that people appear to be comfortable in improvising with them." In a field trial they found that people readily appropriated a range of available objects (including teabags, mobile phones, jewellery, and drinks containers) to act as tangible tokens to be used within the system.

Figure 4.2: An established technological niche.

Creating and retreating into technological niches may be our response to being confronted by the complexity of digital technology characterised as "information overload" (e.g., Klingberg, 2009; Pijpers, 2010) or, more constructively, they may reflect the practice of off-loading the cognitive burden to the environment.

Irrespective of their aetiology, examples of technological niches readily come to mind: the games arcade, the quiet study area, any teenager's bedroom, and the more contingent ephemera around the "water cooler." These contingent niches are the "bubbles" of separateness that surrounds the individual engaged in a phone conversation walking down a busy street, or sitting on a train or relaxation area.

Figure 4.3 is an image of a group of students spontaneously ignoring each other in a relaxation area. Each has used their own technology to create a "bubble" of separateness about themselves.

Figure 4.3: Ad hoc technological niches?

4.9.1   NICHES AND ECOLOGIES

Technological niches are necessarily smaller, simpler, more manageable and more closely aligned to our needs, both personal and professional, than the modern world as a whole or the "world of work." They can be recognised as specialist cognitive ecologies (Tribble and Sutton, 2011). This being so, these niches present themselves as: (i) a more useful partition within larger technological ecologies; and (ii) a meaningful unit of design, evaluation, and description. We can also locate these niches with larger artefact ecologies. Kirsh (1996) has proposed that artefact ecologies comprise five elements—"species", systems, user groups, practices, and the task environment. An artefact "species" might include such things as axes or knives, table or desktop computers, which "compete with" and complement each other; artefact systems are collections or constellations of other mutually related artefacts (e.g., knives and forks). User groups are sub-populations, or communities of practice, which are defined, in part, by the artefacts they use; and practices explain how artefacts are used. Finally, task environment are "the underlying constraints determining what is helpful and unhelpful in accomplishing a task. When a practitioner uses an artefact or system to work towards complete a task—the task environment—that determines how each successful artefact-using step is in bringing the practitioner closer to the goal." Thus we can locate technological niches within this framework as a variety of task environments.

Finally, if creating our own niches proves to be too demanding we can even buy an "off-the-shelf" ready-made niche; for example, it has been observed that certain manufacturers create technological niches (also described as a "walled garden") to ensure that their product range works together seamlessly. Similar observations have been made of social media which effectively shield the individual users from the vagaries of the Web by offering all a user could possibly want within the confines and safety of their own platform. We can add to this list virtual teams, virtual meeting rooms, and a whole host of technological innovations prefixed by the modifier "virtual" which also fall into this broad definition of technological niche. While these ready-made niches may serve many of the same purposes as a bespoke niche, using them is not an act of appropriation (for the reasons given at the beginning of Section 4.6).

4.10 IN SUMMARY

The different accounts of coping considered in Chapter 3 offer compelling descriptions of how we deal with the world as a whole and digital technology in particular. However it is a matter of fact that coping is routinely scaffolded by a range of established and contingent epistemic actions which help ensure that we use digital technology effectively. It will be recalled that by epistemic we mean, "the entire canvas of topics the mind can address: the nature of man-made symbols and culture, and even the simple layout of objects in the immediate environment" (vide Chapter 1) and this certainly seems to be the case in practice. In the next and final chapter of this lecture we locate coping within HCI.

CHAPTER 5

Coping in Context

5.1 KEY POINTS

- Coping fits into contemporary, mainstream accounts of human-computer interaction as while it is both embodied and situated it recognises the importance of using distributed resources to achieve our goals with digital technology.

- Coping adds an account of *how* we use digital technology and as such complements goal- and purpose-oriented models, descriptions, and treatments which address the *what* and *why* of human-computer interaction.

5.2 SITUATED, EMBODIED, AND DISTRIBUTED

At present there is no single, overarching account of HCI, but there are broad themes upon which most researchers would agree are important to any such account. These are that human-computer interaction is situated, embodied, and distributed—there may be others but we will focus on these.

In the preceding chapters we have argued that coping is both situated and embodied and relies upon distributed resources. This being so, coping lies squarely within the corpus of HCI but let us examine each of these claims in turn. As this material has already been covered in detail already we will keep this (mercifully) brief.

5.2.1 COPING IS THE *SITUATED* USE OF DIGITAL TECHNOLOGY

The last ten years or so has witnessed a number of commentators and researchers suggesting that we are on the verge of a paradigm shift within HCI, which I shall call "new wave HCI." This new wave[2] or the "situated perspective" is set to replace the earlier engineering view ("fitting the person to the machine") and the cognitive view ("treating a person as a cognitive machine").

Suchman (1987) introduced the concept of situated interaction to the HCI community specifically as a critique of an aspect of Artificial Intelligence, namely, human-machine communication. She writes, " … I wanted to compare the user's and the system's respective views of the interaction …" (p. 123). Since then, the concept of the situated nature of interaction has been very

---

[2] Some researchers have called this "second wave HCI" (e.g., Bødker, 2006) while others propose a "third wave HCI" (e.g., Bardzell and Bardzell, 2011) and there has even been a hint of a fourth wave. Rather than getting tied up in an argument over numbering, the term "new wave" has been adopted.

widely adopted, appropriated, and variously extended by different groups within HCI to suit their own purposes.

Carroll (2003) reflecting on the impact of Suchman's work observes that it helped expand the outlook of the HCI community, facilitating the subsequent impact of activity theory, participatory design, and ethnographically driven design (p. 273). Yvonne Rogers (2012), writing in this series, echoes these sentiments and concludes that the impact of situated action on HCI was to foreground the importance of *context*. She writes, "it changed the way researchers thought of computer interactions and work activities, taking context to be a focal concern" (p. 47). So, how does this account of coping fit within this description of situated HCI?

1. Coping, from the outset of this lecture, has been described as adaptive and responsive to the situation we find ourselves in. The key to this flexibility is our familiarity with digital technology. This familiarity provides us with a readiness to cope with it rather than to execute a fixed set of responses. Presented with technology we are ready and able to use it.

2. Secondly, coping is routinely scaffolded by making use of the situation itself, that is, the resources in the local environment, the available information and computational resources, the technology itself, other people and so forth.

3. Suchman relegates our reliance on plans to use the technology (that is, plans being the product of our detached deliberations) to the role of resources upon which we can call upon as required.

Coping is situated.

5.2.2 COPING IS THE *DISTRIBUTED* USE OF DIGITAL TECHNOLOGY

Hutchins' account of cognition (1995a; 1995b) offers a radical rethink of the structure and dynamics of cognition. His key proposal is that cognitive processes may both be distributed across multiple human actors, artefacts, internal and external representations of information, social and institutional factors, and across the relationships among these elements as they work to achieve an overall goal. Given these very many "extra-cranial" components he described his account as *distributed cognition*. In the intervening years, distributed cognition has become a familiar concept within HCI though it has remained largely a descriptive one.

As for coping: we have written at length regarding the measures we take to scaffold our use of digital technology. Any and all examples of these epistemic acts rely upon, by definition, resources that lie outwith our brain-based cognition. Kirsh and Maglio themselves (Maglio et al., 2004) have identified *parallels* between their work and a resource-based approach to distributed cognition within the HCI literature (Wright et al., 2000). Parallels perhaps but not equivalence. The issue hinges on whether we fully adopt Clark and Chalmer's position that the use of external representation is functionally equivalent to what happens in the brain *or* we regard them as (mere) adjuncts or scaffolding to our coping. A case could be made for either, but we would suggest that while coping may not be a fully fledged example of distributed cognition, it is certainly consistent with thinking in this area.

Coping is distributed.

5.2.3   COPING IS THE *EMBODIED* USE OF DIGITAL TECHNOLOGY

Being situated and distributed are related, tend to overlap, but are fairly easy to define and apply in this context. Would that it were so when we consider embodiment. In chapter three, we presented a number of different philosophical accounts of coping and noted that all of them would claim that they embraced embodiment. We also noted that the nature of embodiment in cognitive science, philosophy, and HCI remains largely unresolved.

However what we can say is that coping depends upon familiarity, and our familiarity with the world is based on our experiences with it and these, at least initially, are direct and unmediated. As we trace back the origins of our ability to cope with digital technology comes the recognition that this begins and ends with our corporeality.

Coping is embodied.

Finally, a word from Clark (2008, p. 70) who brings together cognition, corporeality, and epistemic actions writing that "... epistemic actions, I want to suggest, are paramount among the ways in which bodily activity yields transient but cognitively crucial extended functional organizations."

5.3   COPING IS HOW WE USE DIGITAL TECHNOLOGY

Table 5.1 is reproduced from Bødker and Klokmose (2012a). From their Activity Theoretic perspective, they identify three levels of analysis that can be applied to purposive, technologically mediated behaviour and the three corresponding analytic questions. And it is these questions which offer the second means of locating this account of coping within HCI as a whole.

Table 5.1: After Bødker and Klokmose, 2012a, p. 202				
Levels of activity	Mental representation	Realises	Level of description	Analytical question
Activity	Motive—not necessarily conscious	Personality	The social and personal meaning of activity …	Why?
Action	Goal—under conscious control	Activities (systems of actions organised to achieve goals)	Possible goals, critical goals, particularly relevant sub-goals	What?
Operation	Conditions of actions—normally not under conscious control	Actions (chains of operations organised by goals and concrete conditions)	The concrete way of executing an action in accordance with the specific conditions surrounding the goal	How?

Beginning at the top of the hierarchy, it is difficult to imagine any better treatment of the motivational level than Activity Theory itself which uniquely brings together motive (as object) and personality in answering the question, *why* are we engaged in this activity.

A step down addresses the action/goal level of analysis which is of particular interest to HCI as it is arguably its primary unit of analysis. From this perspective, we undertake actions (tasks) to achieve goals and to understand the goal of using technology is to answer the question, "What is technology being used for?" It is possible that this level may have received the most sustained attention because it is the most readily available for empirical investigation. Importantly, a task within HCI is an abstraction. A task is, in practice, only a representation of some of the aspects of a task such as its goals and the methods employed to achieve them (Card et al., 1983) or its semantic qualities or "grammar" (Payne and Green, 1990).

By contrast, the lowest level of analysis concerns how the activity is realised. Of this level Activity Theory tells us that this refers to "the concrete way of executing an action in accordance with the specific conditions surrounding the goal." This level is situated, not under conscious control, and approximates to intuitive behaviour and System 1 thinking. Coping is located at this level. Coping is primarily and specifically practical and concrete in nature.

Coping, unlike the higher levels of an activity, is not susceptible to generalisation or abstract. While instrumental detachment has allowed us massive strides forward in physics and chemistry it is not appropriate here. As powerful as this privileged instrumental perspective is, we need to shift our focus back to the everyday concerns of "know-how", involvement, availability, and corporality in order to understand how coping works. Coping is also a re-iteration of the observation that *techne* precedes *episteme*; "knowing-how" comes before "knowing-that", emphasising the former but not dispensing with the latter. And for us, whether theorist or practitioner, "how" is what we need to know in considering digital technologies which are no longer novel or intimidating but are an all too familiar feature of everyday life.

5.4   LAST WORD: A FRESH LOOK AT COGNITIVE SCIENCE?

As I write these last few lines I recall Carroll's observation that "the initial vision of HCI as an applied science was to bring cognitive-science methods and theories to bear on software development" (2003, p. 3). Cognition and cognitive science are a little out of favour with the HCI community and have often been on the receiving end of fairly trenchant criticisms. However it should be recognised that many of these criticisms actually refer to the classical (and rather dated) treatment of cognition, which was concerned with rules and symbol manipulation. It is hoped that this lecture has demonstrated that contemporary cognitive science has a great deal to contribute to our understanding of how we use digital technology and I, for one, would encourage its embrace.

Bibliography

Agre, P. E. (1997). *Computation and Human Experience*. Cambridge University Press. DOI: 10.1017/CBO9780511571169. 6

Akah, B. and Bardzell, S. (2010). Empowering Products: Personal Identity through the Act of Appropriation. Proc. CHI 2010: Work in Progress, 4021-4026. DOI: 10.1145/1753846.1754096. 62

Baber, C. and Stanton, N. A. (1997). Rewritable routines in human interaction with public technology. *International Journal of Cognitive Ergonomics*, 1(4), 237-249. 26

Bærentsen K. B. and Trettvik, J. (2002). An Activity Theory Approach to Affordance. Proceedings of the second Nordic conference on Human-computer interaction, 51-60. DOI: 10.1145/572020.572028. 46

Bakhurst, D. (1991). *Consciousness and Revolution in Soviet Philosophy*. Cambridge: Cambridge University Press. DOI: 10.1017/CBO9780511608940. 25

Bardzell, J. and Bardzell, S. (2011). Pleasure is your birthright: digitally enabled designer sex toys as a case of third-wave HCI. Proceeding CHI '11 Proceedings of the SIGCHI Conference on Human Factors in Computing Systems, 257-266. DOI: 10.1145/1978942.1978979. 69

Belin, A. and Prié, Y. (2012). DIAM : Towards a Model for Describing Appropriation Processes Through the Evolution of Digital Artifacts. Proceedings of DIS '12: Proceedings of the Designing Interactive Systems Conference 2012, June 11-15, 2012, Newcastle, UK, 645-654. DOI: 10.1145/2317956.2318053. 61Bell, G., Blythe, M. and Sengers, P. (2005). Making by Making Strange: Defamiliarization and the Design of Domestic Technologies. *ACM Transactions on Computer-Human Interaction*, 12(2), 149–173. DOI: 10.1145/1067860.1067862. 22

Bentley, R., Hughes J. A., Randall, D., Rodden, T., Sawyer, P,. Shapiro, D., and Sommerville, I. (1992). Ethnographically-informed systems design for air traffic control. CSCW '92 Proceedings of the 1992 ACM conference on Computer-supported cooperative work, 123-129. DOI: 10.1145/143457.143470. 53

Bertenthal, B. I., Rose, J. L., and Bai, D. L. (1997). Perception-Action Coupling in the Development of Visual Control of Posture. *Journal of Experimental Psychology: Human Perception and Performance*, 23(6), 1631-1643. DOI: 10.1037/0096-1523.23.6.1631. 42

Blackler, A. and Hurtienne, J. (2007). Towards a unified view of intuitive interaction: definitions, models and tools across the world. *MMI-Interaktiv*, 13. pp. 36-54. 15, 43

Blackler, A., Popovic, V., and Mahar, D. (2003a). Designing for intuitive use of products. An investigation. Proceedings of 6th Asia Design Conference, Tsukuba, Japan. 15

Blackler, A., Popovic, V., and Mahar, D. (2003b). The nature of intuitive use of products: An experimental approach. *Design Studies*, 24(6), 491-506. DOI: 10.1016/S0142-694X(03)00038-3. 15

Blevis, E. (2007). Sustainable interaction design: invention & disposal, renewal & reuse. In Proceedings of the SIGCHI Conference on Human Factors in Computing Systems (San Jose, California, USA, April 28 - May 03, 2007). CHI '07. ACM Press, New York, NY, 503-512. DOI: 10.1145/1240624.1240705. 61

Blom, J. (2002). A theory of personalised recommendations. Extended abstracts of the CHI 2002 Conference on Human Factors in Computing Systems, New York: ACM. DOI: 10.1145/506443.506471. 63

Blom, J. and Monk, A. (2003). A theory of personalisation: why people personalise their PCs and mobile phones. *Human Computer Interaction*, 18, pp. 193-228. DOI: 10.1207/S15327051HCI1803_1. 63

Bødker, S. (1991). Activity theory as a challenge to systems design. In H-E Nissen, H K Klein and R Hirschheim (Eds) *Information Systems Research: Contemporary Approaches and Emergent Traditions*. Elsevier Science Publishers B. V. (North-Holland), 551-564. 26, 32, 46

Bødker, S. (2006). When Second Wave HCI meets Third Wave Challenges. NordiCHI 2006 The 4th Nordic Conference on Human-Computer Interaction Oslo, Norway — October 14 - 18, 2006, 242-251. DOI: 10.1145/1182475.1182476. 6, 69

Bødker, S. and Klokmose, C. N. (2012a). The Human-Artifact Model – An Activity Theoretical Approach to Artifact Ecologies. *Human-Computer Interaction*. 26(4), 315-371. DOI: 10.1080/07370024.2011.626709. 6, 71, 72

Bødker, S. and Klokmose, C. N. (2012b). Dynamics in artifact ecologies. Proc. NorchiCHI 2012, 448-457.

Borgmann A. (1984). *Technology and the Character of Contemporary Life*. The University of Chicago Press, Chicago. 62

Bowers, J. (1994). The work to make a network work: studying CSCW in action. Proceedings of the 1994 ACM conference on Computer supported cooperative work. 287-298. DOI: 10.1145/192844.193030. 53

Bowers, K. S., Regehr, G., Balthazard, C., and Parker, K. (1990). Intuition in the context of discovery. *Cognitive Psychology*, 22, 72-110. DOI: 10.1016/0010-0285(90)90004-N.

Card, S., Moran, T. P., and Newell, A. (1983). *The Psychology of Human-Computer Interaction*. Hillsdale, NJ: Laurence Erlbaum Associates. 8, 72

Carr, N. (2008). Is Google Making Us Stupid? *Atlantic Magazine*, 301(6). 2

Carr, N. (2010). *The Shallows*. NY: Norton and Company. 2

Carroll, J. M. (2003). Situated action in the zeitgeist of human-computer interaction. *The journal of the learning sciences*. 12(2), 273-278. DOI: 10.1207/S15327809JLS1202_7. 70

Carroll, J. M. (2003). Introduction: Towards a multidisciplinary science of human–computer interaction. In J. Carroll (Ed) *HCI models, theories and frameworks*. San Francisco, CA: Morgan Kaufmann, pp. 1-9. 73

Carroll, J. M. and Carrithers, C. (1984). Training Wheels in a User Interface. *Communications of the ACM*, 27(8), 800-806. DOI: 10.1145/358198.358218. 60

Chase, W. G. and Simon, H. A. (1973). Perception in chess. *Cognitive Psychology*, 4, 55-81. DOI: 10.1016/0010-0285(73)90004-2. 42

Chemero, A. (2009). Radical Embodied Cognitive Science. Cambridge, MA: MIT Press. 38

Clark, A. (1997a). The dynamical challenge. *Cognitive Science*, 21(4), 461–481. DOI: 10.1207/s15516709cog2104_3. 36, 42

Clark, A. (1997b). *Being There: Putting Brain, Body, and World Together Again*. Cambridge: Cambridge University Press. 36, 57

Clark, A. (2001). Reasons, Robots and The Extended Mind. *Mind and Language*. 16(2), 121-145. DOI: 10.1111/1468-0017.00162. 54

Clark, A. (2008). *Supersizing the Mind*. Oxford University Press. 14, 38, 51, 71

Clark, A. and Chalmers, D. J. (1998). The Extended Mind. *Analysis* 58, 10-23. DOI: 10.1093/analys/58.1.7. 38

Clark, A. and Grush, R. (1999). Towards a Cognitive Robotics, *Adaptive Behavior*, 7(1), 5-16. DOI: 10.1177/105971239900700101. 36, 37

Csikszentmihalyi, M. (1990). *Flow: the psychology of optimal experience*. Harper and Row, New York. 33

Csikszentmihalyi, M. (1992). *Flow: the psychology of happiness*. Rider, London. 33

Da Souza, C. S. (2005). *The Semiotic Engineering of Human-Computer Interaction*. Cambridge, MA: MIT Press.

Dalton, N., MacKay, G., and Holland, S. (2012). Kolab: Appropriation & Improvisation in Mobile Tangible Collaborative Interaction. DIS 2012, June 11-15, 2012, Newcastle, UK, 21-24. 64

Davidson, W. L. (1882). Definition of Intuition. *Mind*, 7(26),304-310. DOI: 10.1093/mind/os-VII.26.304. 41

Dawkins, R. (1976). *The Selfish Gene*. Oxford, England: Oxford University Press. 25

Dey, A., Abowd, G., and Salber, D. (2001). A conceptual framework and a toolkit for supporting the rapid prototyping of context-aware applications. *Human-Computer Interaction*, 16(2–4), 97–166. DOI: 10.1207/S15327051HCI16234_02. 32

Dillon, A. and Scaap, D. (1996). Expertise and the Perception of Shape in Information. *Journal of the American Society for Information Science*, 47(10), 786-780. DOI: 10.1002/(SICI)1097-4571(199610)47:10<786::AID-ASI7>3.0.CO;2-Z. 42

Dix, A. (2007). Designing for Appropriation. Proceedings of the 21st BCS HCI Group Conference, Vol.2, 27-30. 2, 61

Dixon, P. and O'Reilly, T. (2002). Appearance, form and the retrieval of prior knowledge. In J Frascara (Ed) *Design And The Social Sciences: Making Connections*. London: Taylor and Francis, 166-177. 15

Donner, J. and Csikszentmihalyi, M. (1992). Transforming stress into flow. *Executive Excellence*, 9, 16-17. 33

Dourish, P. (2003). The appropriation of interactive technologies: Some lessons from placeless documents. *Computer Supported Cooperative Work*, 12, 465–490. DOI: 10.1023/A:1026149119426. 61

Dreyfus, H. L. (1991). *Being-in-the-world: A Commentary on Heidegger's Being and Time, Division 1*. Cambridge, MA: MIT Press. 7, 13

Dreyfus, H. L. (2007). Response to McDowell, *Inquiry*, 50, 371-377. 30

Dreyfus, H. L. and Wrathall, M. A. (2005). Introduction. In H.L. Dreyfus and M.A. Wrathall (Eds) *A Companion to Heidegger*. Malden, MA: Blackwell Publishing. 4

Dreyfus, H. L., Dreyfus, S. E., and Anthanasiou, T. (1988). *Mind Over Machine: The Power of Human Intuition and Expertise in the Era of the Computer*. New York: Free Press. 43

Dreyfus, S. E. and Dreyfus, H. L. (1980). *A Five-Stage Model of the Mental Activities Involved in Directed Skill Acquisition*. Washington, DC: Storming Media. 31

Engeström, Y. (1987). *Learning by expanding: An activity-theoretical approach to developmental research*. Helsinki: Orienta-Konsultit.

Engeström, Y. (1999). Expansive visibilization of work: an activity theoretic perspective, *CSCW - an International Journal*. 8(1-2), 66-92.

Ericsson, K. A. and Simon, H. A. (1984). *Protocol Analysis. Verbal Reports as Data*. Cambridge, MA: MIT Press. 45

Espinosa, J. R. D. and Mares, P. R. (2012). Familiarity of challenges and Optimal Experience in Movement Interaction Games. Proc. MexIHC '12, Mexico city, Mexico, 47-50. DOI: 10.1145/2382176.2382187. 23

Farrow, D. and Abernethy, B. (2003). Do expertise and the degree of perception - action coupling affect natural anticipatory performance? *Perception*, 32(9), 1127 – 1139. DOI: doi:10.1068/p3323. 42

Flyvbjerg, B. (2001). *Making Social Science Matter*. Cambridge, England: Cambridge University Press. 12

Freeman, J., Ijsselsteijn, W., and Lessiter, J. (2000). The Presence Construct: Issues in its Measurement. Proc. 3rd International Workshop on Presence, no page numbers. 23

Galloway, A., Brucker-Cohen, J., Gaye, L., Goodman, E., and Hill, D. (2004). Design for hackability. Proc. DIS'04. ACM Press, New York, NY, 363-366. DOI: 10.1145/1013115.1013181. 61

Gardiner, M. M. and Christie, B. (1987). *Applying Cognitive Psychology To User-Interface Design*. John Wiley & Sons, Inc. New York, NY, USA.

Gibson, J. J. (1977). The Theory Of Affordances. In R. Shaw and J. Bransford, Eds, *Perceiving, Acting and Knowing*. New York: Wiley, 67 - 82. 42

Gibson, J. J. (1979). *The Ecological Approach to Visual Perception*. Boston: Houghton Mifflin. 42

Gibson, J. J. (1986). *The Ecological Approach To Visual Perception*, Lawrence Erlbaum Associates, Hillsdale, NJ. 19, 42

Goldin-Meadow, S., Nusbaum, H., Delly, S., and Wagner, (1991). Explaining Math: Gesturing lightens the load. *Psychological Science*, 12(6), 516-22. DOI: 10.1111/1467-9280.00395. 38

Goldman, A. I. (1986). *Epistemology and Cognition*. Harvard University Press. 8

Goodwin, C. and Goodwin, M. H. (1998). Seeing as a situated activity: Formulating Planes. In Y Engestrom and D Middleton (Eds.) *Cognition and Communication at Work*. Cambridge University Press. 42

Gregor, P., Newell, A. F., and Zajicek, M. (2002). Designing for Dynamic Diversity - Interfaces for Older People. Proc. ASSETS 2002 - The Fifth International ACM Conference on Assistive Technologies, 8-10 July, Edinburgh, 151-156. DOI: 10.1145/638249.638277. 60

Gregory, R. L. (1966). *Eye and Brain: The Psychology of Seeing*. London: Weidenfeld and Nicolson. 34

Gregory, R. L. (1970). *The Intelligent Eye*. London: Weidenfeld and Nicolson. 34

Heath, C. and Luff, P. (1992). Collaboration and Control: Crisis Management and Multimedia Technology in London Underground Line Control Rooms. *Computer-Supported Cooperative Work*, 1(1-2), 69-94. DOI: 10.1007/BF00752451.

Heath, C. and Luff, P. (2000). *Technology in Action*. Cambridge, England: Cambridge University Press. DOI: 10.1017/CBO9780511489839. 58

Heidegger, M. (1927/1962). *Being and Time*. (Translated by J. Macquarrie and E. Robinson) New York: Harper Collins. 5, 7

Heidegger, M. (1971). *The Question Concerning Technology*. In D F Krell (Ed) Basic Writings: Martin Heidegger. London: Routledge, 307-342. 18

Herstad, J. and Holone, H. (2012). Making sense of co-creative tangibles through the concept of familiarity. NordiCHI '12 Nordic Conference on Human-Computer Interaction Copenhagen, Denmark, 89-98. DOI: 10.1145/2399016.2399031. 24

Hollan, J., Hutchins, E., and Kirsh, D. (2002). Distributed Cognition: Toward a New Foundation for Human-Computer Interaction Research. *ACM Transactions on Computer-Human Interaction*, 7, 174 –196. DOI: 10.1145/353485.353487.

Höök, K. (2006). Designing Familiar Open Surfaces. NordiCHI 2006 The 4th Nordic Conference on Human-Computer Interaction Oslo, Norway — October 14 - 18, 2006, 242-251. DOI: 10.1145/1182475.1182501. 23, 24

Hostetter, A. B. and Alibali, M. W. (2008). Visible embodiment: Gestures as simulated action. *Psychonomic Bulletin & Review*, 15(3), 495–514. DOI: 10.3758/PBR.15.3.495. 38

Hurtienne, J. and Israel, J. H. (2007). Image Schemas and Their Metaphorical Extensions – Intuitive Patterns for Tangible Interaction. TEI Tangible and Embedded Interaction 2007 Baton Rouge, LA, USA — February 15 - 17, 2007. DOI: 10.1145/1226969.1226996. 15, 16

Hutchins, E. and Klausen, T. (1996). Distributed Cognition in an airline cockpit. In Y Engeström and D Middleton (Eds.) *Cognition and Communication at Work*. Cambridge University Press, 15-34. DOI: 10.1017/CBO9781139174077.002.

Hutchins, E. (1995a). *Cognition in the Wild*. Cambridge, MA: MIT Press. 70

Hutchins, E. (1995b). How a cockpit remembers its speed. *Cognitive Science*, 19, 265-288. DOI: 10.1207/s15516709cog1903_1. 70

Janlert, L-E. and Stolterman, E. (2010). Complex Interaction. *ACM Transactions on Computer-Human Interaction*, 17(2) Article 8. DOI: 10.1145/1746259.1746262. 6

John, B. E. and Kieras, D. E. (1996). Using GOMS for user interface design and evaluation: Which technique? *ACM Transactions on Computer-Human Interaction*, 3, 287-319. DOI: 10.1145/235833.236050. 8

Jung, H., Stolterman, E., Ryan, W., Thompson, T., and Siegel, M. (2008). Toward a framework for ecologies of artifacts: How are digital artifacts interconnected within a personal life? Proceedings of the NordiCHI 2008. ACM Press. 201-210. DOI: 10.1145/1463160.1463182. 6

Kahneman, D. (2011). *Thinking, fast and slow*. London: Allen Lane. 40

Kaptelinin, V. (1997). Activity Theory: Implications for Human-Computer Interaction. In B. Nardi (Ed.) *Context and Consciousness*, Cambridge, MA: MIT Press, 103-116. 46

Kasabach, C., Pacione, C., Stivoric, J., Gemperle, F., and Siewiorek, D. (1998). Digital ink: a familiar idea with technological might! CHI 98 Conference Summary on Human Factors in Computing Systems, 175-176. DOI: 10.1145/286498.286654. 23

Kirsh, D. (1995a). The intelligent use of space. *Artificial Intelligence*, 73, 31-68. DOI: 10.1016/0004-3702(94)00017-U. 54, 55

Kirsh, D. (1995b). Complementary strategies: Why we use our hands when we think. In Johanna D. Moore and Jill Fain Lehman (Eds) Proceedings of the Seventeenth Annual Conference of the Cognitive Science Society, 212-217. 38

Kirsh, D. (1996). Adapting the environment instead of oneself. *Adaptive Behaviour*, 4(3/4), 415-452. DOI: 10.1177/105971239600400307. 66

Kirsh, D. (2010). *Explaining Artifact Evolution. Cognitive Life of Things: Recasting the Boundaries of the Mind*. Cambridge University Press. 63

Kirsh, D. and Maglio, P. (1994). On distinguishing epistemic from pragmatic action. *Cognitive Science*, 18, 513-549. DOI: 10.1207/s15516709cog1804_1. 2, 9, 51

Klemmer, S. R., Hartmann, B., and Takayama, L. (2006). How bodies matter: five themes for interaction design. Proceedings of the 6th conference on Designing Interactive Systems, June 26-28, University Park. PA, 140-149. DOI: 10.1145/1142405.1142429. 38, 51

Klingberg, T. (2009). *The Overflowing Brain: Information Overload and the Limits of Working Memory*. OUP USA. 65

Koriat, A. and Goldsmith, M. (1996). Memory metaphors and the real-life/laboratory controversy: Correspondence versus storehouse conceptions of memory. *Behavioral and Brain Sciences*, 19(2), 167-228. DOI: 10.1017/S0140525X00042114.

Kuutti, K. (1996). Activity Theory as a Potential Framework for Human-Computer Interaction research. In B Nardi (Ed.) *Context and Consciousness*, Cambridge, MA: MIT Press, 17-44. 46,

Lakoff, G. and Johnson, M. (1999). *Philosophy in the Flesh*. NY: Basic Books. 16

Laland, K. N. and Sterelny, K. (2006). Perspective: seven reasons (not) to neglect niche construction. *Evolution*, 60(9), 1751-1762. DOI: 10.1111/j.0014-3820.2006.tb00520.x. 63

Lave, J. (1977). Cognitive Consequences Of Traditional Apprenticeship Training In West Africa. *Anthropology & Education Quarterly*. 8(3), 177–180. DOI: 10.1525/aeq.1977.8.3.05x1512d. 55

Lim, K.H., Benbasat, I. and Todd, P.A. (1996). An Experimental Investigation of the Interactive Effects of Interface Style, Instructions, and Task Familiarity on User Performance. ACM Transactions on Computer-Human Interaction, 3(1), 1–37. 22

Lim, B-C., and Klein, K. J. (2006). Team mental models and team performance: a field study of the effects of team mental model similarity and accuracy. *Journal of Organizational Behavior*, 27(4), 403–418. DOI: 10.1002/job.387.

Mackay, W. E., Fayard, A-L., Frobert, L., and Médini, L. (1998). Reinventing the Familiar: Exploring an Augmented Reality Design Space for Air Traffic Control. Proc. CHI '98. 558-565. DOI: 10.1145/274644.274719. 23

MacLean, A., Carter, K., Lövstrand, L., and Moran, T. (1990). User-tailorable systems: pressing the issues with buttons. CHI '90 Conference on Human Factors in Computing Seattle, WA, USA — April 01 - 05, 1990. ACM Press, 175-182. 61

Maglio, P. P., Wenger, M. J., and Copeland A. M. (2004). The Benefits of Epistemic Action Outweigh the Costs. Proceedings of the 25th Annual Cognitive Science Society: Part 1 and 2 (Cognitive Science Society (US) Conference. R Alterman and D Kirsch (Ed). Lawrence Erlbaum Associates Inc. 70

Magnani, L. and Bardone, E. (2008). Sharing Representations and Creating Chances through Cognitive Niche Construction. The Role of Affordances and Abduction. *Studies in Computational Intelligence (SCI)* 123, Springer-Verlag Berlin Heidelberg, 3–40. 52, 63

Malone, T. W. (1983). How do people organize their desks? Implications for the design of office automation systems. *ACM Transactions on Office Systems*, 11, 99-112. DOI: 10.1145/357423.357430. 53, 54, 59

May, R. (1996). (trans. G Parkes). *Heidegger's Hidden Sources: East-Asian Influences on his Work*. Oxford, England: Rouledge. 33

McCarthy, J. and Wright, P. (2004). *Technology as Experience*. Cambridge, MA: MIT Press.

McDonnell Corporation (1965). *NASA Project Gemini Familiarization Manual*. St. Louis, Missouri. 24

McGonagall, J. (2011). *Reality is Broken*. London: Jonathan Cape. 2

Montagne, G., Buekers, M., Camachon, C., de Rugy, A., and Laurent, M. (2003). The learning of goal-directed locomotion: A perception-action perspective. *The Quarterly Journal of Experimental Psychology*: Section A, 56(3), 551 – 567. DOI: 10.1080/02724980244000620. 42

Moore, A. and O'Neill, K. (2001). *The League of Extraordinary Gentlemen*. DC Comics, New York, NY, USA. 62

Murrell, K. F. H. (1965). *Ergonomics – Man In His Working Environment*. London: Chapman and Hall. 17

Nardi, B. (1996). Some reflections on the application of activity theory. In B Nardi (Ed.) *Context and Consciousness*, Cambridge, MA: MIT Press. 46

Neisser, U. (1978). Memory: What are the important questions? In M M Gruneberg, P Morris and R Sykes (Eds) *Practical aspects of memory*. London: Academic Press, 3-24.

Nelson, H. and Stolterman, E. (2003). *The Design Way – Intentional Change in an Unpredictable World*. Educational technology Publications. New Jersey. 61

Newman, M. W., Sedivy J. Z., Neuwirth, C. M., Edwards, W. K., Hong, J. I., Izadi, S., Marcelo, K., and Smith, T. F. (2002). Designing for Serendipity: Supporting End-User Configuration of Ubiquitous Computing Environments. DIS 2002 Designing Interactive Systems 2002. 61

Noddings, N. and Shore, P. J. (1984). *Awakening the inner eye intuition in education*. Columbia University: Teachers College Press. 43

Norman, D. A. (1981). Categorization of Action Slips. *Psychological Review*, 88(1), 1-15. DOI: 10.1037/0033-295X.88.1.1. 45

Norman, D. A. (1983). Some observations on mental models. In D. Gentner & A. Stevens (Eds.) *Mental Models*. Hillsdale, NJ, USA: Lawrence Erlbaum Associates. 8

Norman, D. A. (1988). *The Psychology of Everyday Things*. New York: Basic Books. 8

Norman, D. A. (2004). *Emotional design: Why we love (or hate) everyday things*. New York: Basic Books. 41

Norros, L. (2005). The concept of habit in the analysis of situated action. *Theoretical Issues in Ergonomic Science*, 6(5), 385-407. DOI: 10.1080/14639220500076520. 7

Payne, S. J. and Green, T. R. G. (1990). Task Action Grammar: recent developments. In D Diaper (Ed.) *Approaches to Task Analysis*. Cambridge University Press. 72

Payne, S. J. (1991). A Descriptive Study Of Mental Models. *Behaviour and Information Technology*, 10, 3-21. DOI: 10.1080/01449299108924268. 37

Pierce, C. S. (1931 – 1958). *Collected Papers of Charles Sanders Peirce*. Cambridge, MA: Harvard University Press. 52

Pijpers, G. (2010). *Information Overload: A System for Better Managing Everyday Data*. Wiley. 65

Pollard, W. (2006). Explaining Actions with Habits. *American Philosophical Quarterly*, 43, 57-68. 7

Polyani, M. (1983). *The Tacit Dimension*. Peter Smith, Gloucester, MA. 12, 14

Prensky, M. (2001). Digital Natives, Digital Immigrants. *On the Horizon*, 9(5). Lincoln: NCB University Press. 3

Qin, H., Rau, P. L. P., and Salvendy, G. (2009). Measuring Player Immersion in the Computer Game Narrative, *International Journal of Human-Computer Interaction*, 25(2), 107-133. DOI: 10.1080/10447310802546732. 23

Raskin, J. (1994). Intuitive Equals Familiar. *Communications of the ACM*. 37(9), 17. DOI:10.1145/182987.584629. 43

Rasmussen, J. (1983). Skills, rules, and Knowledge; signals, signs and symbols, and other distinctions in human performance models. *IEEE Transactions on Systems, Man, and Cybernetics*, Vol.smc-13, No. 3, 257-266. DOI: 10.1109/TSMC.1983.6313160. 45

Rauscher, F. H., Krauss, R. M., and Chen, Y. (1996). Gesture, Speech, And Lexical Access: The Role of Lexical Movements in Speech Production. *Psychological Science*, 7(4), 226-231. DOI: 10.1111/j.1467-9280.1996.tb00364.x. 39

Reason, J. and Mycielska, K. (1982). *Absent-minded?* Englewood Cliffs, NJ: Prentice-Hall, Inc. 43

Riva, G. and Mantovani, F. (2012). From the body to the tools and back: a general framework for Presence in mediated interactions. *Interacting with Computers*, 24(4), 203-210. DOI: 10.1016/j.intcom.2012.04.007. 39, 40

Rizzolatti, G. and Sinigaglia, C. (2008). *Mirrors in the Brain: How Our Minds Share Actions, Emotions, and Experience*. Oxford: Oxford University Press. 17

Rogers, Y. (2012). *HCI Theory: Classical, Modern, and Contemporary*. Morgan & Claypool Publishers. 70

Rogers, Y. and Ellis, J. (1994). Distributed Cognition: an alternative framework for analysing and explaining collaborative working. *Journal of Information Technology*, 9(2), 119-128. DOI: 10.1057/jit.1994.12.

Rogoff, B. (1984). Introduction: Thinking and learning in social context. In B Rogoff and J Lave (Eds.) *Everyday Cognition: Its Development In Social Context*. Cambridge, MA: Harvard University Press, 1–8. 44

Rouse, J. (2000). Coping and Its Contrast. In M. Wrathall and J. Malpas (Eds.) *Heidegger, Coping, and Cognitive Science*. Cambridge. MA: MIT Press. 30

Rowe, P. G. (1991). *Design Thinking*. Cambridge, MA: MIT Press. 52

Ryan (2009). Device Ecology Mapper: A Tool for Studying Users' Ecosystems of Interactive Artifacts. CHI EA '09 Extended Abstracts on Human Factors in Computing Systems, 4327-4332. DOI: 10.1145/1520340.1520661. 6

Salovaara, A. (2008). Inventing New Uses For Tools: A Cognitive Foundation For Studies On Appropriation. *Human Technology*, 4(2), 209–228. 61

Scaife, M. and Rogers, Y. (1996). External Cognition: How Do Graphical Representations Work? *International Journal of Human-Computer Studies*, 45, 185- 213. DOI: 10.1006/ijhc.1996.0048. 50

Schaal, S. (1999). Is imitation learning the route to humanoid robots? *Trends in Cognitive Science*, 3(6), 233-242. DOI: 10.1016/S1364-6613(99)01327-3. 42

Schank, R. C. and Abelson, R. (1977). *Scripts, Plans, Goals, and Understanding*. Hillsdale, NJ: Earlbaum Associates. 13

Schmidt, K. and Bannon, L. (1992). Taking CSCW Seriously: Supporting Articulation Work, *Computer Supported Cooperative Work*, 1(1-2), pp. 7-40. 53

Schmidt, K. and Simone, C. (1996). Coordination Mechanisms: Towards a Conceptual Foundation of CSCW Systems Design. *Computer Supported Cooperative Work*, 5, 155-200. DOI: 10.1007/BF00133655. 53

Schneider, W. and Shiffrin, R. (1977). Controlled and automatic human information processing: 1. Detection, search and attention. *Psychological Review*, 84(1), 1- 66. 45

Schneider, W., Dumais, S. T., and Shiffrin, R. M. (1984). Automatic and control processing and attention. In R Parasuraman, and D R Davies (Eds) *Varieties of Attention*. London: Academic Press. 1-27. 45

Scribner, S. (1986). Practical Thought. In R J Sternberg and R K Wagner (Eds.) *Practical Intelligence*. Cambridge: Cambridge University Press, 13-30. 44

Shapiro, L. (2011). *Embodied Cognition*. Routledge: Oxford, England. 38

Shiffrin, R. and Schneider, W. (1977). Controlled and automatic human information processing: Ii perceptual learning, automatic attending and a general theory. *Psychological Review*, 84(2), 127-190. DOI: 10.1037/0033-295X.84.2.127. 45

Silverstone, R. and Haddon, L. (1996). Design and the domestication of information and communication technologies: technical change and everyday life. In R Mansell and R Silverstone (Eds) *Communication by Design: The Politics of Information and Communication Technologies*, OUP, NY, pp. 44-74. 61

Simonton, D. K. (1980). Intuition and analysis: A predictive and explanatory model. *Genetic Psychology Monographs*, 102, 3-60. 43

Smith, D. C. (1985). Origins of The Desktop Metaphor: A Brief History. Panel Presentation. The Desktop Metaphor as an Approach To User Interface Design. CHI '85 Proceedings of the SIGCHI Conference on Human Factors in Computing Systems, 548-549. 15

Stößel, C. (2009). Familiarity as a Factor in Designing Finger Gestures for Elderly Users. MobileHCI '09 Proceedings of the 11th International Conference on Human-Computer Interaction with Mobile Devices and Services. Article No. 78. DOI: 10.1145/1613858.1613950. 23

Streitz, N. A. (2008). From cognitive compatibility to the disappearing computer: experience design for smart environments. ECCE '08 Proceedings of the 15th European conference on Cognitive ergonomics: the ergonomics of cool interaction. Article No. 1. DOI: 10.1145/1473018.1473020. 32

Suchman, L. (1987). *Plans and Situated Actions: the problem of human-machine communication*. Cambridge: Cambridge University Press. 14, 69

Sudnow, D. (2001). *Ways of the Hand: A Rewritten Account*. Cambridge, MA: MIT Press. 57

Sutton, J., Mcilwain, D., Christensen, W., and Geeves, A.. (2011). Applying Intelligence To The Reflexes: Embodied Skills And Habits Between Dreyfus And Descartes. *Journal of the British Society for Phenomenology*, 42(1), 78-103. 50, 57

Tanenbaum, J., Tanenbaum, K., and Wakkary, R. (2012). Steampunk as Design Fiction. Proc CHI'12, May 5–10, 2012, Austin, Texas, USA, 1583-1592. DOI: 10.1145/2207676.2208279.

Thelen, E. and Smith, L. (1994). *A Dynamics Systems Approach to the Development of Cognition and Action*. Cambridge, MA: MIT Press. 42

Thomson, D. G. (1878). Intuition and Inference. *Mind*, 3(11), 339-349. DOI: 10.1093/mind/os-3.11.339. 39

Tolmie, P., Pycock, J., Diggins, T., MacLean, A., and Karsenty, A. (2002). Unremarkable Computing. CHI'02 Human Factors in Computing Systems Minneapolis, MN, USA, 399-406. DOI: 10.1145/503376.503448. 6

Tomasello, M. (1999). *The Cultural Origins of Human Cognition*. Cambridge, MA: Harvard University Press. 17

Tribble, E. B. (2011). *Cognition in the Globe: Attention and Memory in Shakespeare's Theatre*. New York: Palgrave MacMillan. 55

Tribble, E. B. and Sutton, J. (2011). Cognitive Ecology as a Framework for Shakespearean Studies, *Shakespeare Studies* 39, 94-103. 55, 66

Turner, P. (2005). *Affordance As Context. Interacting With Computers*. 17(6), 787-800. DOI: 10.1016/j.intcom.2005.04.003. 25

Turner, P. and Van De Walle, G. (2006). Familiarity as a Basis of Universal Design. *Journal of Gerontechnology*. 5(3), 150-159. 19

Turner, P., Turner, S., and Van De Walle, G. (2007). How Older People Account for their Experiences with Interactive Technology. *Behaviour and Information Technology*. 26(4), 287-296. DOI: 10.1080/01449290601173499. 19

Turner, S. P. (1994). *The Social Theory of Practices: Tradition, Tacit Knowledge and Presuppositions*. Cambridge: Polity Press. 7

Tversky, B. (1993). Cognitive maps, cognitive collages, and spatial mental models. In A. V. Frank and I. Campari (Eds) *Spatial information theory: A theoretical basis for GIS. Berlin*. Springer-Verlag. DOI: 10.1007/3-540-57207-4_2. 17

Valera, F. J. (1992). *Ethical Know-How*. Stanford CA: Stanford University Press. 7, 34, 35

Valera, F. J., Thomson, E., and Rosch, E. (1991). *The Embodied Mind: Cognitive Science and Human Experience*. MIT Press, Cambridge, MA. 30, 34

Verbeek, P-P. (2005). *What Things Do*. Penn State Press. 4, 5

Vygotski, L. S. (1978). *Mind in Society: The Development of Higher Psychological Processes* (English Translation Ed. M Cole) Cambridge MA: Harvard University Press. 58

Vygotski, L. S. (1986). *Thought and Language*. MIT Press, Cambridge, MA. Translated and edited by Alex Kozulin. 58

Wang, Q. and Nass, C. (2005). Less Visible and Wireless: Two experiments on the effects of microphone type on users' performance and perception. CHI '05 CHI 2005 Conference on Human Factors in Computing Systems Portland, OR, USA — April 02–07, 2005. 39

Warren, W. H. (1984). Perceiving affordances: Visual guidance of stair climbing. *Journal of Experimental Psychology: Human Perception and Performance*, 10, 683–703. DOI: 10.1037/0096-1523.10.5.683. 13

Wartofsky, M. (1979). *Models: Representation And Scientific Understanding*. Reidel Publishing Company, Dordrecht, Holland. 42

Weiser, M. (1991). The computer for the 21st Century. *Scientific American*. 265(3), 94-104. DOI: 10.1038/scientificamerican0991-94. 5

Wells, M. (2000). Office clutter of meaningful personal displays: the role of office personalization in employee and organizational well-being. *Journal of Environmental Psychology*, 20, 239-255. DOI: 10.1006/jevp.1999.0166. 54, 63

Westcott, M. R. (1968). *Toward A Contemporary Psychology of Intuition*. New York: Holt, Rinehart and Winston. 41

Wheeler, M. (2004). Is language the ultimate artifact? *Language Sciences*, 26, 693–715. 36

Wheeler, M. (2005). *Reconstructing the Cognitive World*. Cambridge, MA: MIT Press. 7, 35, 36,57

Whitehead, A. N. (1925/ 1997). *Science and the Modern World*. New York: Free Press. 36

Wilson, M. (2002). Six views of embodied cognition. Psychonomic Bulletin & Review, 9(4), 625-636. 37

Winograd, T. and Flores, F. (1986). *Understanding Computers and Cognition*. Norwood, HJ: Ablex Publishing Corp. 5

Wisneski, C., Ishii, H., Dahley, A., Gorbet, M., Brave, S., Ullmer, B., and Yarin, P. (1998). Ambient displays: Turning architectural space into an interface between people and digital information. Proceedings of the First International Workshop on Cooperative Buildings. Vol. 1370, Springer, pp. 22–32. 6

Worden, A., Walker, N., Bharat, K., and Hudson, S. (1997). Making Computers Easier for Older Adults to Use: Area Cursors and Sticky Icons. CHI '97 ACM Conference on Human Factors & Computing Systems. Atlanta, GA, USA — March 22 - 27, 1997. DOI: 10.1145/258549.258724. 60

Wrathall, M. A. (2005). *How to read Heidegger*. Granta Books. 18

Wright, P., Fields, R., and Harrison, M. (2000). Analysing human-computer interaction as Distributed Cognition: The resources model. *Human Computer Interaction*, 51, 1-41. DOI: 10.1207/S15327051HCI1501_01. 70

Zang, N., Rosson, M. B., and Nasser, V. (2008). Mashups: Who? What? Why? Proc. Conference on Human Factors in Computing Systems, extended abstracts on Human factors in computing systems. Florence, Italy - April 05 - 10. 3171-3176. 61

WEB REFERENCES

Agre, P.E. (1985). Routines. *AI Memo 828*. MIT AI Laboratory. Available from http://dspace.mit.edu/bitstream/handle/1721.1/5631/AIM-828.pdf?sequence=2 [last retrieved 25th June 2013]

BBC 2012 [last retrieved 26th June 2013] http://www.bbc.co.uk/news/uk-politics-20539715 **59**

Blevis, E. and Stolterman, E. (2007). Ensoulment and Sustainable interaction design. Proceedings Of The International Association Of Societies Of Design Research 2007: Emerging Trended In Design Research. Available from http://www.sd.polyu.edu.hk/iasdr/ [last retrieved 25th June 2012] 41, 61

BRIO [latest retrieved 23rd February 2013] http://www.brio.net/en/ToPlay/0-18months/My_Very_First.aspx **3**

Dewey, J. (1922). *No separate instincts, Human Nature and Conduct: An Introduction to Social Psychology*. New York: Modern Library, pp.172-180. Available from http://www.brocku.ca/MeadProject/Dewey/Dewey_1922/Dewey1922_15.html [last retrieved 12th June 2013] 7

Ilyenkov, E. (1977). *Problems of Dialectical Materialism* (Translated by A. Bluden) Progress Publishers. Available from http://www.marxists.org/archive/ilyenkov/works/ideal/ideal.htm [last retrieved 11th June 2013] 25

James, W. (1890). *The Principles of Psychology*. Available from http://psychclassics.yorku.ca/James/Principles/index.htm [last retrieved 12th June 2013] 6

Kant, I. (1748). *The Critique of Pure Reason*. Available from http://www.gutenberg.org/ebooks/4280 [last retrieved 23rd June 2013] 41

Kahneman, D. (2002). Maps Of Bounded Rationality: A Perspective On Intuitive Judgment And Choice. Nobel Prize Lecture. http://www.nobelprize.org/nobel_prizes/economics/laureates/2002/kahnemann-lecture.pdf [last retrieved 12th June 2013] 40, 41

Titchner, E. B. (1928). *A Textbook of Psychology*. Available from http://archive.org/details/textbookofpsycho00edwa [last retrieved 28th March 2013] 24

Weiser, M., Brown, J.S. *The coming age of calm technology*. Available from http://www.johnseelybrown.com/calmtech.pdf [last retrieved 15th June 2013] 5

Author Biography

Dr Phil Turner is Reader in Human-Computer Interaction at Edinburgh Napier University. His primary research interest is the development of a theoretically rich understanding of our everyday experience of interactive technologies. Phil has published widely in this domain, drawing on insights from cognitive science, philosophy, and psychology during his two decades of work in both industry and latterly academia.

Printed in the United States
by Baker & Taylor Publisher Services